THE PERSONALITY OF EMERSON

THE PERSONALITY OF
EMERSON

BY F. B. SANBORN

HASKELL HOUSE PUBLISHERS Ltd.
Publishers of Scarce Scholarly Books
NEW YORK. N. Y. 10012
1971

First Published 1903

HASKELL HOUSE PUBLISHERS Ltd.
Publishers of Scarce Scholarly Books
280 LAFAYETTE STREET
NEW YORK, N. Y. 10012

Library of Congress Catalog Card Number: 72-156911

Standard Book Number 8383-1290-X

Printed in the United States of America

PREFATORY NOTE

HAVING *determined to write a series of volumes describing the personal traits of four distinguished authors whom I intimately knew,—Emerson, Thoreau, Ellery Channing, and Bronson Alcott,—I offer this volume as the second. So close were the relations of these friends, that mention of all is naturally made in each book, involving some repetition. From these books, illustrated with portraits, a good conception is had of the Concord school of poets and philosophers, who were so distinctly original.*

A part of the plan was to give in each book the best portrait, with a facsimile of manuscript. The portrait of Thoreau did not appear in "The Personality of Thoreau," but was reserved for Channing's life. Emerson's portrait here given was painted by David Scott at Edinburgh in 1848, but reached America thirty years later, and was never well engraved before. In some respects it is the best of many portraits.

F. B. S.

CONCORD, February 14, 1903.

A LIMITED EDITION of five hundred copies of this book was printed on French hand-made paper, and twenty-five copies on Japan paper, by D. B. UPDIKE, THE MERRYMOUNT PRESS, BOSTON, in March, 1903. This is copy Nᵒ.

THE PERSONALITY OF EMERSON

In writing of my comparatively short acquaintance with Henry Thoreau, I was easily able to recall the circumstances under which I first became
acquainted, not only with his person, but with his
mind. It was not so in my relations with Emerson; for so early did I begin to read his writings,
that I can hardly remember when I did not know
them, at least superficially. A natural affinity for
the school of thought which he most clearly rep-
resented, and something akin to his intuitions in
my own way of viewing personal and social matters, brought me into relations with him long before I ever saw him, or heard that thrilling voice
which few who had listened to its deeper tone
could ever forget. I was indeed as much younger
than Emerson as Persius was younger than his
revered Stoic philosopher, Cornutus; but I could
have said, and often did say to myself, after be-
coming intimate with the Concord philosopher,

[1]

what young Persius proclaimed in lasting Latin
verse:—

> *" Nescio quod certe est, quod me tibi temperat astrum."*
>
> 'T was sure some star attuned my fate to thine.

I must have begun to read Emerson before six-
teen; for in my sixteenth year I remember perus-
ing with indignation Francis Bowen's review of
the *Poems*, which came out in the *North American Review* for 1847; and it was soon after that
I first made Carlyle's acquaintance in his early
book, *Sartor Resartus.* The second edition of Emerson's *Nature* came in 1849, when I was seventeen; and at eighteen I had read the *Essays*, and
the remarkable biographical criticism of Plato,
Shakespeare, Montaigne, and Napoleon in *Representative Men.* But the little town where I was
born and spent all these earliest years, with the
exception of a few weeks at Boston in 1843,
though abounding in good books and inspiring
teachers, hardly ever attracted a lecturer of more
than local repute; and Exeter, its market-town
and seat of learning, had no inclination to invite
Transcendentalists to its "Lyceum." I remember

in my nineteenth year, as I was reading Greek
with Professor Hoyt of the Exeter Academy, he
related to me how his classmates at Dartmouth
invited Emerson in 1838 to give them that grand
discourse on *Literary Ethics* which was one of
the first of his orations I had read, how few understood it, and how Emerson repelled the proposal
of reporting it. "I curse the Reporters," said the
gentle sage,—"I curse them"; so, at least, my old
teacher reported that Emerson at Hanover had
said to him. But when, many years after, I cited
this remark to Emerson, he could not believe he
had made it. But his opinion was so constant,—
that the casual reporter is sure to misunderstand
and misreport,—and he had suffered so often
therefrom, that I never really doubted the exact
memory of Professor Hoyt. Singularly enough,
Emerson disliked even the exact reporter, though
for a different reason, of course. He was almost
morbidly sensitive about repeating his essays to
those who had read them in full; thinking it de-
prived him of their fresh attention, and lost them
the interest of surprise, on which his rhetoric so

largely depended at the first hearing. In the last decade of his life he gave in Concord that essay on *Eloquence* which came out shortly before his death, in the volume called *Letters and Social Aims,*—a title that gave him much trouble, like the definition of "civilization." It was new to me, in February, 1875, and I knew it would be pleasing to readers of the *Springfield Republican.* I therefore took full notes, and spent the next day or two in looking up the orators he had quoted,— Lafayette, John Quincy Adams, and Canning,— and was fortunate enough to find the very page from which he had copied a remarkable address of Lafayette to the Chamber of Deputies (June 21, 1815), in which he threw down the gauntlet to Napoleon.

As Emerson, for some reason, omitted it from his volume, and it may be unknown to my readers, I will quote it as Emerson read it to us at the Concord "Lyceum":—

"Napoleon, returning from Elba, was obliged to summon a Chamber of Deputies, and among them came Lafayette. When Napoleon came back from Waterloo to Paris, he resolved to abolish this Assembly. Lafayette heard of it. In the first session afterward he ascended the tribune without delay, and said: 'When for the first time in many years I raise in this Chamber a voice *which the friends of free institutions will recognize,* I feel myself called upon, Gentlemen, to address you respecting the dangers of the country, which you alone are now able to save. Sinister reports have been spread abroad; they are now unhappily confirmed. The moment has arrived for rallying around the old tri-colored standard of 1789,—the standard of liberty, equality, and public order. Permit, Gentlemen, a veteran in this sacred cause, one who was ever a stranger to the spirit of faction, to submit to you some resolutions,—the necessity of which, I trust, you will feel as I do. Let this Assembly declare itself in permanent session; let it send for the ministers of State, and require of them a report on the present aspect of affairs.' The Assembly voted as Lafayette had proposed. Then Lucien Bonaparte, who was a deputy, rose in his place, bowed to Lafayette with profound respect, and left the hall. In two hours Napoleon sent in his abdication."

But to my story. When this report appeared, five days after, in my newspaper, Emerson saw it and was grieved. He met me in the street and said, "You should not have reported my quotations. Dog must not eat dog." I explained my reasons; but they did not convince him; he wished to use that lecture again, and thought this report hindered him.

It was not till I entered Harvard College, in the summer of 1852, that I had opportunities of hearing and meeting Emerson. I had heard Theodore Parker in the year before; but in April, 1851, when I visited Boston for the second time, and Concord for the first time, Emerson was not making public addresses, in the week or ten days at my disposal; and though I passed his house, whose door stood invitingly open (his daughter Ellen descending the stairway, reminding me of some angel in Allston's *Jacob's Dream*), I had not then the courage to call on him. I did so for the first time in July, 1853, after hearing him

lecture occasionally, and after meeting Alcott,
Parker, Mrs. Cheney, and others of his friends. I
had walked up from Cambridge to Concord over
the Turnpike, on my way to visit Henry Shaw, a
former schoolmate, in Sudbury. Reaching Emerson's house, at the corner where the Cambridge
Turnpike debouches into the Lexington road
(now Massachusetts Avenue), about eleven in
the morning, I rang the bell and was shown at
once into the study, where Emerson sat in his
accustomed chair, facing the Fates of Michel
Angelo over the mantel. He was either reading
or writing, as his morning habit was. I had no
letter of introduction, but perhaps used the name
of some mutual friend, Alcott or Parker; was
received graciously, and questioned about the
young men in College, where I had just ended
my Sophomore year, with some small tokens of
distinction among classmates, — a Society Poem,
or something of the kind. I observed that, after
giving me one of those gently piercing glances
which took in so much of the character of his
visitors, he did not look directly at me in ques-

tioning or replying; but gazed at one side, as if withdrawing his mind from persons to ideas. What I remember best of his remarks is his hoping to see a "good crop of mystics at Harvard," —the last place in which many of that class were to be found, or had been, for some years.

Emerson was then in the vigor of middle age, just turned of fifty, in good health and fine color, with abundant dark brown hair, no beard, but a slight whisker on each cheek, and plainly dressed. His form was never other than slender, after I knew him, and his shoulders, like Thoreau's, had that peculiar slope which had attracted notice in England, where the New England type of Anglo-Norman was not so well known as it has since become. His striking features were the noble brow, from which the hair was carelessly thrown back, though not long, and the mild and penetrating blue eye, smiling, in its social mood, in the most friendly manner, but capable, on rare occasions, of much severity. The portrait by David Scott, painted at Edinburgh five years before, erred by giving him a complexion and an eye too dark; but in its general expression was then almost perfect; and five years later, in 1858, Rowse drew and threw aside an unfinished head which best preserves the noble serenity of his gaze.

From the date of this visit, although at first I saw Emerson but seldom, I felt at ease in his company, except in those moments which all his intimates experienced (and some of them bitterly lamented and complained of), when he seemed to be removed to an infinite distance from human companionship, and hardly to recognize the presence of those with whom he seemed to be conversing. This trait, or circumstance,—for it must have been a part of his fate, rather than an element in his disposition, which was eminently social and friendly,—I was wont to explain by his superiority of nature, which of necessity isolated him from those around him, until by the force of will and generosity he brought himself within the daily round of common thoughts and cares, in which he did not naturally belong. His was the higher poetic nature, to which the phenomenal world presents itself as a phantasm rather than a fact, and from which the daily events and companionships of life seem strangely averse and remote. The ecstasies and profundities of religious and philosophic meditation are akin to this poetic exaltation; and all were mingled and exemplified in some of those experiences which Emerson has himself narrated, and which appeared also in the solitary and thoughtful spiritual life of his eccentric aunt, Mary Moody Emerson. To her, as he was wont to say, he was much indebted for his early induction into the graver paths of self-culture. The typical passage on this matter in Emerson's books is that which occurs so early in the first one, his philosophic abridgment called *Nature*, where he says of himself: "All mean egotism vanishes. I become a transparent eye-ball; I am nothing, I see all; the currents of the Universal Being circulate through me; I am part or parcel of God. The name of the nearest friend sounds then foreign and accidental: to be brothers, to be acquaintances,—master or servant, is then a trifle and a disturbance."

This abstraction and aloofness of mind, if its

powers are once turned toward human things, gives extreme clearness of vision and appreciation. Emerson said of himself, "I have the fatal gift of perception"; and those who saw much of him soon learned to understand this, without always knowing from what quality in his nature so remarkable a gift proceeded. Simplicity had something to do with it, and the poetic eye much more. George Chapman, himself a poet of no mean order, in dedicating his version of Homer to Lord Howard of Walden, said well of Poesy, personified: —

"Virtue, in all things else at best, she betters,
　　Honor she heightens, and gives life in death;
　She is the ornament and soul of letters;
　　The world's deceit before her vanisheth:
　Simple she is as doves, like serpents wise,
　　Sharp, grave and sacred; nought but things divine
　And things divining fit her faculties, —
　　Accepting her as she is genuine."

This saying could hardly be applied in literal strictness to any man; but it came near to the higher moods of Emerson. He had also a practical side, which often puzzled those who expected to find him all sage or all poet, and perceived instead an unusual versatility or even worldliness. This is said to have been less noticeable before his second visit to England in 1847–48, which was some years earlier than I saw him; it was recognized, however, by Lowell in his clever portrayal of Emerson in the *Fable for Critics*, which first appeared in 1848:—

> "A Greek head on right Yankee shoulders, whose range
> Has Olympus for one pole, for t'other the Exchange;
> A Plotinus-Montaigne, where the Egyptian's gold mist
> And the Gascon's shrewd wit cheek-by-jowl coexist;
> He sits in a mystery calm and intense,
> And looks coolly around him with sharp common-sense."

When I first knew him, in the years 1853–56, the long conflict over the questions of American slavery was shaping itself for final decision by the ordeal of battle; and Emerson had taken his public attitude on it some ten years earlier,—a fact which for a time escaped the notice of his friend and correspondent Carlyle, who was inclining to the support of negro slavery, from his contempt for the African, and his worship of force.

It was about this time, say in 1854, when I had become a frequent visitor at Theodore Parker's hospitable house in Exeter Place, Boston, that he told me the story of his own colloquy with Carlyle on this point, in the Chelsea house, in 1843, at an evening conversation when Doctor John Carlyle was present, and several contemporaries were discussed. Parker found the two Carlyles sitting round the open fire, where on the hob was the kettle heating for the Scotch beverage of whiskey punch. At first, literature was the theme, and Tennyson, then just rising into note as a poet, though he had been long known to Emerson, in the early edition of 1833, which, bound in red morocco, used to lie on Emerson's table. Parker, who was not so good a judge of poets as of theologues, began to give Carlyle his notion of Tennyson, as an exquisite who arrayed himself for writing verse in a silk-lined dressing-gown, and, seated at an inlaid table, with a gold-tipped quill, would indite verses on satin paper, like "Airy, fairy Lilian" or *Claribel*. Carlyle laughed loud at the picture. "Ow, that 's not so at all,—Alfred comes here and drinks his toddy and smokes his pipe like the rest of us; he's no dandy nor milksop." America then coming up for consideration, Carlyle began to rail against "Quashee" and the Abolitionists, whose cause Parker championed, of course. But Carlyle said, "Your neighbor Emerson's no Abolitionist; he thinks about these things much as I do." "On the contrary," said Parker, "he no longer withdraws from association with active reformers, like Garrison, but is outspoken against negro slavery." Carlyle could hardly believe it. "But," said Parker to me, "when I reached home in 1844, and Emerson had printed that trenchant address on *West India Emancipation*, which Mrs. Brooks, Mrs. Emerson, and the Thoreaus made an occasion for him to give in Concord (August 1, 1844), I had the satisfaction of sending the pamphlet to Carlyle at Chelsea." It contained this passage, among others, which indicates how the slave question addressed itself to Emerson when I first knew him:—

"As I have walked in these pastures and along the edge of woods, I could not keep my imagina-

tion on agreeable figures, for other images that
intruded on me. I could not see the great vision
of the patriots and senators who have adopted the
slave's cause,—they turned their backs on me.
No: I see other pictures,—of mean men: I see
very poor, very ill-clothed, very ignorant men, not
surrounded by happy friends,—to be plain, poor
black men of obscure employment as mariners,
cooks or stewards in ships, yet citizens of this
our Commonwealth,—freeborn as we, whom the
slave-laws of South Carolina have arrested in ves-
sels, and shut up in jails. This man, these men,
these men I see, and no law to save them. . . .
Gentlemen, I thought the deck of a Massachusetts ship was as much the territory of Massachusetts as the floor on which we stand. It should be
as sacred as the temple of God. If such a dam-
nable outrage can be committed on the person of
a citizen with impunity, let the Governor break
the broad seal of the State; he bears the sword
in vain."

No doubt Emerson was thinking of the crest
and legend on the State seal of our State,—the

arm with uplifted sword grasped in a firm hand, picturing the first half-line of Algernon Sidney's inscription in the table-book of the King of Denmark,—while the legend gave the other line, promising freedom to all who might come under our flag:—

" Manus hæc, inimica tyrannis,
Ense petit placidam sub libertate quietem."

This device and motto, selected by John Adams, who framed our first State Constitution, and presided at its revision, forty years after, I once translated thus:—

This hand, the tyrant's foe,
Seeks peace, through freedom, with a manly blow.

Emerson had a great admiration for both the Adamses, John and John Quincy; he once told me that John Adams was in his view the greatest of the Revolutionary patriots,—superior to Franklin or Jefferson, and, though not Washington's equal in moral qualities or military talent, a far better writer. Washington, he said, was a heavy writer, and against Jefferson he had retained some of the prejudices of the Boston Fed-

eralists, in which he had grown up. His brother
Edward, who died early in Porto Rico, was tutor of some of the elder Adams's grandsons, and
Waldo Emerson liked to relate the visit the two
brothers made to the old statesman at Quincy; he
read it to me from his journal of February, 1825,
before he included it in his essay on *Old Age*.
They found the old President in his easy-chair,
calmly awaiting the death that found him there
the next year. When they asked him about his
son, who had just been chosen President, he
praised the political prudence of John Quincy
Adams, but said, "I shall never see him again; he
will not come to Quincy but to my funeral; it
would be a great satisfaction to me to see him,
but I don't wish him to come on my account."
He lived to see his son more than once, though
ninety years old in 1825. When I related to Emerson a story of Adams in his old age, which I had
from Theodore Parker, and he from Reverend
Doctor Gray of Roxbury, he refused to believe it,
such was his veneration for John Adams; though
the anecdote was quite in keeping with his well-

known' irascibility. Doctor Gray was invited to dine with the ex-President at the house of a parishioner, and, as Mr. Adams was leaving early, the Doctor stepped into the hall to help him on with his overcoat. Then ensued this colloquy:—

Adams. I thank you, Doctor Gray, for your polite attention.

Gray. Do not mention it, Mr. Adams; no attention is too great, no trouble is too much, that we of this century have the privilege of taking for the patriots of the Revolution,—for General Washington and yourself, Sir.

Adams. Do not name Washington to me, Sir! Washington was a dolt!

"No," said Emerson, "I cannot believe that story;" nor would he, when I gave him my authority. He loved also to cite the eloquence of John Quincy Adams, which he has described in one of his essays. Indeed, he was a follower of eloquent men, and once told me that he reported a great speech of Harrison Gray Otis, then reckoned Boston's chief orator, and was complimented by Otis on his accuracy. He had in truth a re-

[18]

markable verbal memory, as all poets should have; since much of their easy writing of verse depends upon it.

Quincy Adams was dead and gone before I ever saw Emerson; so was Webster before I ever conversed with him; but Emerson liked to commemorate those earlier days, before Webster made his *gran rifiuto*, in 1850, and went to his grave in 1852 under the heavy censure of the best sentiment in Massachusetts. It was to Emerson that Carlyle in 1839 wrote his remarkable word-portrait of Webster in England, which the Concord friend allowed Webster's biographers to copy, and which disclosed the unhandsome as well as the glorious features of his character. In 1845, when Webster and Choate came to Concord for a week, to defend the fraudulent bank officer (against whose offence there was then no countervailing law), and got him acquitted, Mrs. Emerson, who remembered Webster in black dress-coat and small-clothes at the Plymouth Pilgrim festival of 1820, where he made one of his noblest orations, gave a reception for Webster and the gentlemen of the Middlesex Bar, of which the leader was then Samuel Hoar of Concord, father of Senator Hoar. Edward Emerson, before his health gave way, and he went to the West Indies in the hope of restoration, had been the tutor of Webster's sons, and had studied law in the great man's Boston office. But the flaw in the metal of Webster did not escape the piercing insight of Emerson, long before he betrayed his trust on the slavery question. He told me one or two anecdotes of Webster's chronic insensibility to the demands of honor where money was concerned,—one of them dating back before 1830; and when the March speech of 1850 came to shatter the hopes of Webster's anti-slavery friends, whom he should have led instead of deserting, Emerson wrote in his journal:—

"Why did all manly gifts in Webster fail?
He wrote on Nature's noblest brow, For Sale."

He also, just before I made his personal acquaintance, gave a public address, at Cambridge and elsewhere, in which he portrayed the scope of Webster's mind, and the lack of moral greatness in the man so grandly endowed; but he would never publish it, and it has never appeared in full.

Of Waldo Emerson's brothers, to whom he was most tenderly attached, I saw only William, the eldest, and Bulkeley, the "innocent,"—who, though a bright and capable child up to the age of ten or twelve, then had his mental growth arrested by some severe malady, and continued through a long life to be dependent on others for his care and comfort. While I knew him, he resided in Littleton, a few miles west of Concord, adjoining Harvard, where his father, Reverend William Emerson, had his first parish, and where many of the descendants of Reverend Peter Bulkeley, the founder of Concord in 1635, were then living. William Emerson was a lawyer of success in New York City, with a house on Staten Island before I knew him, in which Thoreau lived for a time in 1843, as the tutor of his three sons, and where Ellery Channing, during his short residence in New York as one of the editors of the *Tribune*, under Horace Greeley, used to visit. I soon met William Emerson at his brother's house in Concord, and when I first visited New York, in the spring of 1856, I dined at his city house, and heard from him the story of his interview with Goethe in 1825, or about that time. Emerson had early told me of this, and that, when the young American, who was destined for the pulpit, like his ancestors for many generations, laid before the German sage his religious doubts, and sought counsel whether he should preach or not, Goethe advised him to swallow his scruples and preach. The conscientious Christian could not do this; he returned to his mother's Roxbury home in October, 1825, and saddened her by giving up his purpose of entering the ministry, beginning the study of law soon after. He was a faithful, courteous, but slightly formal gentleman, well read and affectionate, but rather antipathetic to Thoreau and the more eccentric Transcendentalists. I also knew for a few years that noteworthy aunt of the Emersons, Miss Mary Moody Emerson, the youngest child of Emerson's grandfather, who built the Old Manse, where she was born; and she used to say "she was in arms

at Concord Fight" because her mother (who had
a brother and cousins on the Tory side) held her
up at the window to see the redcoats as they
marched past the Parsonage on their way to the
historic North Bridge. She was therefore more
than eighty when I met her at her nephew's fire-
side,—a small, energetic, by no means beautiful
person, but of singular talents and much originality, which had been of great service to the
children of her deceased brother, as they grew up
under her eye. Like her nephew, she had great
regard for beautiful persons,—men, women, or
children,—and equally good esteem for original
persons, though they might hold opinions which
she abhorred. Thoreau was such a person; and
her interest in him, which he reciprocated, gave
a piquancy to their interviews, and to her comments on him, made to me and others. She did
not accept Bronson Alcott in the same way,
though admiring his fine aspect and graceful
manners. When she first heard him explain his
new system of instruction for children, which he
was then exemplifying in Boston, she wrote to

him (October 30, 1835) thus:—

"While the form dazzled,—while the speaker inspired confidence,—the foundations of the— the—superstructure, gilded and golden, was in depths of,—I will tell you plainly what, when I am furnished more with terms as well as principles. No marvel that Age is at a loss to express itself about a system, theory or whatever, which is proposed for Infancy. If you will have the kindness to send me a letter including the Conversation, and as much more as you can afford, I will, if you give leave, express myself more plainly, on a ground which now seems to give way to my literality and common-sense philosophy. It will gratify me if you will read a book which I left for you at Front Street, 13. It is an antidote to your opinions, and is modern Unitarianism of a higher order; and I know no one whom I wish to read it more than yourself."

Having administered this courtly reproof, Miss Mary gave the needful sugar-plum at the close of her letter: "Mr. Emerson came to welcome me home; but he talked of nothing but the pleasure

of seeing you. Affectionate regards to Mrs. Alcott, and hearty wishes for your success." Three
years later, when the "tempest in a wash-bowl,"
as Emerson styled it, over his Divinity Hall Address of 1838 was raging, this proud and loving,
but controversial, aunt of his wrote to her half-
brother, Reverend Samuel Ripley of Waltham
(who had married her dearest young friend, Miss
Sarah Bradford), as follows:—

[No year date, but presumably 1839,—the postage six cents.]

"BELFAST, 18 (Sabbath ev'g) November.

"MY DEAR BROTHER:

" *The pleasure of hearing of your clerical arrangements by the Reg-*
" *ister last week makes me write for very gladness. What time will*
" *be given you,—and how desirable to unite the sheep into one fold!*
" *A subject which I have waited since Sarah's conversation in the*
" *Vale* [*Old Manse*] *to know about, with no little interest. And God*
" *forbid that you preach as you write to me, when expatiating on the*
" *virtues of those whose Christian faith is broken up into the glitter-*
" *ing fragments of a corrupted philosophy and pantheistic specters!*
" *Talk of Waldo's virtues,—I know and respect them,—so had*
" *Spinoza and Fichte and Kant* [*virtues*]. *And they were and are*
" *the gifts of that Being who may be said to laugh at their chimeras.*
" *To talk of a holy life and benevolence, as you do, unless those*
" *virtues are based on the personal Infinite, is like mistaking the me-*

[25]

" teors of night for the lamp of day. The constitution of man for-
" bids it,—history proves it,—and Revelation must be left out of
" the question to profess it. It is true that the fine feelings and in-
" stincts may prevail in the high and pleasant places for a time;
" but even these have received their charms from that divine phi-
" losophy which they are outshining.

" No,—the only basis of all virtue must be (so divinely consti-
" tuted is our poor nature, with all its awful capacity for sin)—
" that we are capable of loving supremely the Infinite; and on that
" capacity is engrafted all benevolent principle: while the criterion
" of virtue in its highest state must always be, that one would not
" sin, were the Deity never to know it. But is it not to obedience unto
" His moral law guiding our conscience, that we owe this love of
" Truth, Justice, Benevolence,—three divine attributes? Is it not
" thro' a personification of them in Jesus that we have been enlight-
" ened, and the charms of these modern philosophers have been thus
" derived? I continue to desire the correspondence of Norton and
" Ripley,—especially as I have read Furness, and with delight, at
" some glimpses he catches of our Master: while his theory is often
" upset by facts. He is an idealist, perhaps, and must stand some-
" what tottling. And Ware's sermon I should like to borrow, and
" the Edin. Review for Oct. 1829. There is a woeful scarcity of
" books (modern) here. Let Waldo know of the means of sending,
" if you chance to see him. And now, dear S., farewell! preach as at
" Waltham; the day and the hour of Sabbath excitement I remember
" with sad pleasure. Love to Sarah, whose brilliant and comprehen-
" sive subjects Lizzie [Ripley] tells me about.

" Your aff. Sister,   M. M. E.

"Say not a word of the contents of this to Waldo, as you
"would be true to me. *I have also a letter to him by the same*
"*mail, and forgot to name the means of writing, etc.*"

It was this lady who, admiring the brilliant wit
of Talleyrand,—not unlike her own, except that
hers was crowded with devout imaginings,—said
with a sigh, "I fear he is not organized for a
future state." Her nephew Waldo, whom she
trained and inspired, and whom she did not wish
to pain by her censures written to his Uncle Ripley, once said of her,—"Her wit was so fertile,
and only used to strike, that she never used it for
display, any more than a wasp would parade his
sting." He told me that "she was in her time the
best writer in Massachusetts"; and he gave this
parallel in a public lecture, largely made up of
his Aunt Mary's writings:—

"When I read Dante the other day, and his
paraphrases to signify with more adequateness
Christ or Jehovah, whom do you think I was reminded of? Whom but Mary Emerson and her
eloquent theology?"

Twenty years or so after this thrust at Al-

cott's theories and her nephew's Transcendental-
ism, I saw her rise up in Emerson's parlor and in-
veigh with sudden vehemence and success against
what she thought the antinomian declarations
by Henry James, Senior, setting at naught the
moral law, and replying to Alcott and Thoreau,
in a set conversation, with some of his usual para-
doxes. It was in December, 1858, and Thoreau
thus sketched the scene in one of his letters to
Harrison Blake:—

"I met Henry James the other night at Emerson's, at an Alcottian conversation, at which, however, Alcott did not talk much, being disturbed
by James's opposition. The latter is a hearty man
enough, with whom you can differ very satisfac-
torily, both on account of his doctrines and his
good temper. He utters quasi-philanthropic dog-
mas in a metaphysic dress; but they are, for all
practical purposes, very crude. He charges society
with all the crime committed, and praises the
criminal for committing it. But I think that all
the remedies he suggests out of his head,—for he
goes no farther, hearty as he is,—would leave us

about where we are now."

The question is as new and fresh to-day as it was when Mary Emerson,[1] with her citations from the Bible and Doctor Samuel Clarke, denounced the smiling and much-amused James for his lax notions,—clasping her hands and raising them above her head, with its odd fillet of black silk, worn to conceal a scar. Enthusiasm, tempered by decorum, seems to have been the mark of the Emerson family; for I have heard Mrs. Sarah Ripley tell how, in the Boston house where the clergyman's widow, assisted by Mary Emerson, was feeding, clothing, and training her orphan sons, Charles Chauncy Emerson, sitting in his low chair near his aunt, while her caller was talking, would start up and interpose a remark, excited by the subject they were discussing, and would need to be quieted by the good lady.

Of this brother Charles I have heard Emerson speak, but not so much as of his older brother Edward, already mentioned, the handsomest and most brilliant (by report) of this noted family. Doctor Holmes, in his first long poem, read at

Harvard College, mentioned Charles Emerson and his then recent death, and again, in addressing the Historical Society after Waldo Emerson's death in 1882, he said with much feeling:—

"Of Charles, the youngest brother, I knew something in my college days; a beautiful, high-souled, pure, exquisitely delicate nature, in a slight but finely wrought mortal frame. He was for me the very ideal of an embodied celestial intelligence. Coming into my room one day, he took up a copy of Hazlitt's *British Poets,* opened it to the poem of Andrew Marvell, *The Nymph Complaining for the Death of her Fawn,* and read it to me, with delight irradiating his expressive features. I felt, as many have felt after being with his brother Waldo, that I had entertained an angel visitant. The Fawn of Marvell's imagination survives in my memory as the fitting image to recall this beautiful youth; a soul glowing like the rose of morning with its enthusiasm,—a character white as the lilies in its purity."

It must have been some three years after this that Charles Emerson, visiting his grandfather's

Concord, Aug. 19. 1830

My Dear Grandfather

My Vacation was almost
gone, & I did not like to have it
wholly pass away, without a visit
here — So I came, although not
sure of finding you at home.
I was in hopes of seeing you (as
your brother mentioned you had
written there was a prospect
of your being at home earlier than
you at first intended) Tuesday
evening. But Tuesday is passed
& it is now Thursday, & I must
bid Goodbye to Concord for the present. I have enjoyed myself

very much — I was pleased
to find your brother & niece
so well & so willing to have
the trouble of a stranger. I
have also enjoyed the sight
of good friends, on whom I have
called — Mr. Geo. Bradford & I
attended the Exhibition yes-
terday at the Academy. We
were extremely gratified —
To hear little girls saying their
Greek Grammar, & young ladies
read Xenophon, was a new
& very agreeable entertainment.
    I am in hopes to see you,
Sir, at Commencement, & am
    ever your affectionate
        & dutiful grandson
            Chas. C. Emerson

Old Manse before Waldo went there to write his first book, *Nature*, wrote the accompanying letter to Doctor Ripley, whose house had been the resort of the brothers in their youth, and for whom they cherished a warm affection. It will interest from the rarity of his writings, of which but few have been printed by his more famous brother, and from the allusion made in it to the teaching of Greek to girls at that early date in Concord. One of the "young ladies" was doubtless Miss Elizabeth Hoar, to whom in after years Charles was affianced.

This acquaintance begun with Waldo Emerson in the summer of 1853 soon became intimacy. In college with me, though in an earlier class, were the son of his boy-companion and schoolmate, the late Doctor Furness of Philadelphia,—now illustrious as the Shakespearian scholar and editor, Doctor Horace Furness,—and his two classmates, Charles Russell Lowell, better known as General Lowell, the nephew of the poet, who died in Sheridan's famous fight near Winchester, in 1864, and the late John Bancroft, elder son of Bancroft the historian. Emerson invited the four of us to dine with him in Concord in May, 1854, and we visited the town together for that purpose. The occasion was a very pleasant social one; but what dwells most in my recollection, from the oddity of the incident, is the fact that on our way through the village to the Emerson residence we found the dead walls near the old tavern (Middlesex Hotel) placarded with caricatures and inscriptions derogatory to Doctor Bartlett, the good old physician who was the leading total-abstinence citizen, and who had been prominent in a recent closure of the hotel bar, where liquors were dispensed contrary to law. This would not have been so noticeable, were it not that among the caricatures and opprobrious words was one great sheet attacking "Rev. R. W. E.," who had been a supporter of Doctor Bartlett in his procedure. This was the day, it seems, which Doctor Edward Emerson, who succeeded Doctor Bartlett for a few years as the village physician, commemorates in his volume, *Emerson in Concord*, as the only instance of any incivility offered

to Emerson in the town which he honored by
his residence for nearly half a century. Doctor
Emerson says:—

"It was the practice of the bar-room wits to
revenge themselves for Doctor Bartlett's coura-
geous and sincere war upon their temple, by
lampooning him in doggerel verse. One morning
there was a sign hung out at the Middlesex stable
with inscription insulting to Doctor Bartlett. Mr.
Emerson came down to the Post Office, stopped
beneath the sign, read it, and did not leave the
spot till he had beaten it down with his cane. In
the afternoon when I went to school I remember my mortification at seeing a new board hang-
ing there, with a painting of a man with a tall
hat, long nose, and hooked cane raised aloft; and
lest the portrait might not be recognized, the
inscription ran, 'Rev. R. W. E. knocking down
the Sign.'"

As Edward Emerson was then but ten years
old, his memory may be a little at fault; for the
caricature, as I recall it, was a rough charcoal
sketch, and the Bartlett inscriptions, which had

been renewed, were on pasteboard, nailed to the side of the tavern stable which abutted on the sidewalk across the "Mill Dam," as the short street of shops was then called, because laid out over what had been the village miller's grist-mill dam in Revolutionary days. Of course, we college students respected the village lampoon.

There had been an earlier gathering of students from Cambridge in the Emerson drawing-room in October, 1853, to listen to a conversation, in which, I believe, Bronson Alcott was the leader, as he was in May, 1854, when a similar company gathered there. Of this October conversation I have but a dim remembrance, having made no record of it, as I did in the one following. In May, 1854, while most of the party went to Concord by train, four of us walked up along the Cambridge Turnpike, and this walk and the following talk I reported, a few days later, in writing Miss Walker, then at Keene, New Hampshire, who was as ardent an Emersonian and Platonist as myself. It was on a Saturday, and the record runs thus:—

"At half-past nine in the morning we started from the Colleges to walk up. It was hot at first, and we went with coats and cravats off until we got within two or three miles of the house of 'The Sage,' as Frank Barlow, who once lived in Concord, calls Mr. Emerson. We walked fast, through a beautiful country (Cambridge and Lexington mostly), on a lonely road, passing near the birthplace of Theodore Parker, and beguiling the way with talk. The distance is thirteen miles, and we were four hours on the road. By one o'clock our stomachs began to hint of dinner, and, as we had not been thoughtful enough to bring any luncheon, and there were no taverns since stage-coaches ceased to run there, we fell to asking for food at the farm-houses in Concord. Three times we were refused; but at last, within sight of the Emerson house, we came to an Irishman's cottage, which had been the home of Ellery Channing ten years before, where the woman of the house was busy painting her kitchen with her own hands. We wished to be able to say, when questioned by Mr. Emerson, that we had dined; and as this was our last opportunity, we urged our request there; and, though it was at great inconvenience to herself, the good woman (Mrs. Shannon) gave us a meal of bread and butter and milk, —the milk, she told us, from the Emerson cows. We ate heartily with young appetites, while she was lamenting she had no better fare to offer. 'I'm shure, boys, it is dreadful that I am so all in a mess here, with the paintin',—and you been walkin' so far,' said she with the kindest of smiles. We told her it was all we needed,—that we were going on to Mr. Emerson's, a neighbor of hers. 'Ah yes! and the best neighbor I ever had he is too,'—and went on to praise him in good earnest. Hawthorne she remembered, two or three years back, when he lived at the Wayside; but she did not speak so highly of him. Coming away, we offered to pay her, but she refused, and when we were going to give it to her little boy, he also refused the money. We left it on the table; whereupon the lad said with as much dignity as an earl could show, 'Mother, the gentleman has left some money on our table,—I'm sure I don't know what it's for.'   [36]

EMERSON

"By two o'clock we got to Mr. Emerson's—
past the hour set for the conversation,—and it
began at once, Emerson being fond of punctual-
ity. At first it was about Cambridge and Harvard
College and the choice of a profession: Could literature be a young man's occupation? Mr. Emerson said: 'It has formerly been the opinion that
literature by itself will not pay; but it seems now
that this omnivorous passion for lectures, review
articles, and other things within the capacity of
scholars, has at last made it easy for a man in England or America to be a scholar and nothing else,
—as Thomas Carlyle is. All men of power and
originality make their own profession nowadays,—
for example, Theodore Parker, Mr. Alcott, here,
Charles Brace, with his practical philanthropy,
and even Albert Brisbane of New York, who be-
lieves in stellar duties, and introduced Fourierism
into this country, after aiding Doctor Howe to
be released from his Prussian prison twenty years
ago. He told me once that he had the good fortune to silence Carlyle,—a great thing, if it were
true,—but Carlyle may have been only bored by

our countryman, who is a sad button-holder. The
railway train is the place to talk with Brisbane,
where time is long, and at your own disposal.'
Then we talked of the Cambridge professors,—
of Longfellow and his destined successor, J. R.
Lowell, who had become acquainted with Emerson when he was 'rusticated' from the class of
1838, and studied in Concord with Reverend Mr.
Frost, the parish minister,—and of the Harvard
system of instruction and restriction. Emerson
thinks rhetoric is now too much neglected there; it
was better taught under Professor Edward Channing, who trained a whole generation to be good
writers, and sometimes good speakers,—such as
Wendell Phillips. Something led the talk toward
Shakespeare, and then it became more deeply interesting to me. I spoke of the deep mystery of
Shakespeare's genius,—so much poetry and philosophy and dramatic power, in one of whose life
and training we know so little,—quoting some of
the sayings of Emerson in *Representative Men.*
Some one brought out the curious fact that,
though he uses the language of Christianity a few

times, as in *Measure for Measure* and *Henry IV*, there is so little Christianity in him you would hardly guess from his plays and poems that he lived among Christians,—and his dear friend Marlowe was denounced in his short life as an atheist. Emerson said 'Shakespeare was a pagan in the best sense of that word'; and quoted Jones Very (the religious devotee, who wrote a remarkable essay on *Hamlet*) as saying, 'If I can move Shakespeare I can move the world,—and already I begin to see him shake a little.'

"Mr. Alcott, who was visiting Emerson, his home now being in Boston, had sat in silence all this time; but now Mr. Emerson asked his view of Shakespeare's religion. Mr. Alcott began with a Socratic question,—'Is not the reason why we of this day see no religion in him, because he was the only religious man whom the Anglo-Saxon race (not much addicted to religion) has yet produced among its writers? Many others have had an alien religion,—have ingrafted the Hebrew religion upon themselves, as our Puritans did,— wherefore Jewry yet leads us in chains. But in

Shakespeare Jewry has no share; his religion is of the blood and the race, and so will only be understood by such as are fine enough to appreciate him in this matter.'

"This was a thought wholly new to us all, especially to three or four students of divinity from the Hall where Emerson in 1838 gave his Divinity School Address. Mr. Alcott went on to expand his idea,—that to each race there is a religion given, peculiarly its own, and modified by its temperament and experiences, as was the Hebrew faith. But these race-religions are the same in their great essentials, and we of the Anglo-Saxon race are now waiting for ours. Emerson followed this thought up by saying: 'When we shall have got what every man nowadays is seeking,—a Bible which can unite the faiths of all mankind,— Shakespeare's sayings will have a large place in it. The ethics of Shakespeare are vast and rich.'

"This led naturally to some talk on pulpit preachers. Emerson said, 'In Great Britain I heard no preaching to compare with ours in America; they have no man there like our Chan-

ning, who was the king of preachers.' He did not
hear Chalmers, the great Scotch preacher, when
he was in Edinburgh in 1847–48; but had heard
Carlyle's early friend, Edward Irving, and posi-
tively disliked him. Again we talked of poets and
other authors,—of Beaumont and Fletcher, the
English metaphysicians, and of Charles Kingsley and his novels, chiefly *Hypatia.* Mr. Alcott
introduced that topic; but it seems Mr. Emerson
does not admire Kingsley, though he has not read
him much. His reading in novels is not extensive,
and he does not always read what Hawthorne
writes. Of poesy he said, 'We do not expect poets
to come from culture; they come from Heaven,'
and he proceeded to inquire whom we have seen
in college, thus sent."

Our party on this occasion, from Cambridge,
was ten in number, of whom, after fifty years,
only three or four survive: Mr. B. S. Lyman of
Philadelphia, Mr. James Hosmer, the well-known
author, now of Minneapolis, myself, and another
whose name escapes me. The latest to die was
my dear friend, Edwin Morton, of Plymouth, a

townsman of Mrs. Emerson, a musician and poet, who spent his last quarter-century in Switzerland, and died at Morges on Lake Geneva in 1900. When Emerson asked that searching question about college poets, Morton was friendly enough privately to name me as one; whereupon Emerson expressed a wish to see some of my verses, with which Morton supplied him. They had been written at Exeter, two or three years before, and printed in a New Hampshire newspaper,—for which I occasionally wrote, from the age of eighteen,—except one poem called *Patience*, which a partial friend had caused to be printed in a Boston journal. He had seen these before this May party, and was good enough to speak kindly of those he had seen, and to request me to send him others. He praised an invective appeal to Daniel Webster, urging him to atone for his apostasy on the slavery question of March 7, 1850, which must have been written that year, before I was nineteen. It was in the iambic measure of Pope and Dryden, and was praised by Emerson—for what, I do not now recall. Another was in praise of Kossuth, when visiting New England, and was written a year or two later, perhaps about the time Emerson was welcoming the Hungarian leader in April, 1852, to the first battle-ground of the Revolution—an address now but little known, in which Emerson said:—

"The people of Concord share with their countrymen the admiration of valor and perseverance; they, like their compatriots, have been hungry to see the man whose extraordinary eloquence is seconded by the splendor and solidity of his actions. But, as it is the privilege of this town to keep a hallowed mound which has a place in the story of the country; as Concord is one of the monuments of freedom; we knew beforehand that you could not go by us. You could not take all your steps in the pilgrimage of American liberty, until you had seen with your eyes the ruins of the bridge where a handful of brave farmers opened our Revolution. Therefore we sat and waited for you. We think that the graves of heroes around us throb to-day with a footstep that sounded like their own:—

[43]

THE PERSONALITY OF

'The mighty tread
Brings from the dust the sound of Liberty.'

Far be it from us, Sir, any tone of patronage; we ought rather to ask yours. You, the foremost soldier of freedom in this age—it is for us to crave your judgment. Who are we that we should dictate to you? You have won your own. We only affirm it. You have earned your own nobility at home. We admit you *ad eundem*, as they say at college. We admit you to the same degree, without new trial. You may well sit a doctor in the college of Liberty. You have achieved your right to interpret our Washington. And I speak the sense not only of every generous American, but the law of mind, when I say that it is not those who live idly in the city called after his name, but those who, all over the world, think and act like him, who can claim to explain the sentiment of Washington.

"We are afraid that you are growing popular, Sir; you may be called to the dangers of prosperity. Hitherto you have had in all countries and in all parties only the men of heart. I do not

[44]

know but you will have the million yet. But remember that everything great and excellent in the world is in minorities. Whatever obstruction from selfishness, indifference, or from property (which always sympathizes with possession) you may encounter, we congratulate you that you have known how to convert calamities into powers, exile into a campaign, present defeat into lasting victory."

My verses, in their small youthful way, expressed the same sentiment as this master of eloquence did soon after; and they had his approval for that, if not for their form. On the *Patience* he made this single criticism; it began

> In the high Heaven, home of endless glee,
> Sits a bright angel at the Father's knee;

upon which touch of affectation he said, "Your use of 'glee' and 'knee' in the beginning was hardly like Michel Angelo." He remembered enough of my versification two years after to ask me to write for the dedication of Sleepy Hollow Cemetery "an ode that can be sung," and I complied. Twenty years later, in 1875, he printed in

his *Parnassus* this ode, and my *River Song*, together with two sonnets describing his daughter
Ellen, and taking for their text Emerson's own
sentence, addressed, I have heard, to Caroline
Sturgis amid her suitors,—"O Maiden! come into
port bravely, or sail with God the seas." As my
verses described with some fidelity a remarkable
character among maidens of the years before our
Civil War, I may be pardoned for quoting them.
The only title I gave them, when sending them
to Emerson, being *Anathemata* (Offerings at a
Shrine), he asked me when about to print them
in his collection, what meaning I attached to the
Greek word, and I gave that above.

I

With joys unknown, with sadness unconfessed,
 The generous heart accepts the passing year,
Finds duties dear, and labor sweet as rest,
 And for itself knows neither care nor fear.
Fresh as the morning, earnest as the hour
 That calls the noisy world to grateful sleep,
Our silent thought reveres the nameless Power
 That high seclusion round thy life doth keep:
So, feigned the poets, did Diana love
 To smile upon her darlings as they slept;

Serene, untouched, and walking far above
  The narrow ways wherein the many crept,
Along her lonely path of luminous air
She glided, of her beauty unaware.

II

Yet if they said she heeded not the hymn
  Of shepherds gazing heavenward from the moor,
Or homeward sailors, when the waters dim
  Flashed with long splendors, widening toward the shore;
Nor wondering eyes of children cared to see;
  Or glowing face of happy lover upturned,
As late he wended from the trysting-tree,
  Lit by the kindly lamp in heaven that burned;
And heard unmoved the prayer of wakeful pain,
  Or consecrated maiden's holy vow,—
Believe them not! they sing the song in vain;
  For so it never was, and is not now.
Her heart was gentle as her face was fair,
With grace and love and pity cloistered there.

But to return to our May party (May 20, 1854). At the close of our formal conversation, tea was served by Mrs. Emerson, after which six of the party were taken by that lady to her "pleached garden," where she showed her blossoming flowers, and gave us bouquets of them. Near by we saw the famous Summer House built by Bronson Alcott while Emerson was abroad in 1847–48, then in good condition, with its harp-adorned gable, and its upper room, to which you mounted by a rustic stairway, winding round the west end, inside; and which stood for perhaps ten years after our visit, and was sketched by Miss Sarah Clarke, Allston's one pupil, from the interior. It was a picturesque addition to the orchard and garden. Delaying too long in this delightful spot, we lost our train on the Fitchburg railroad, and, being unable to find a carriage to take us to the College that evening, the six of us separated,— Morton and Lyman waiting for a later train, while Barlow, Barker, Carroll, and I walked home down what is now Massachusetts Avenue, leaving Barker, a divinity student (afterwards an army chaplain), at East Lexington, where his friend Clarke (a pupil of mine in Greek) was to preach the next day in Doctor Follen's church, and reaching our rooms after midnight.

I have dwelt at some length on this golden day in our college year, because it illustrates so well the unselfish interest which Emerson took in the young men who found in his writings in-

spiration and solace. We were in a feeble minority,—perhaps fifty among the five hundred who
then were registered at Cambridge as students
of Harvard,—the medical students, of whom my
elder brother, the late Doctor C. H. Sanborn of
New Hampshire, was then one, being lodged and
taught in Boston exclusively. We could therefore
cordially agree with Emerson's dictum to Kossuth,—that "everything great and excellent in the
world is in minorities." Among us for a time was
that Oxford scholar, Matthew Arnold's "Thyrsis,"
who had come to New England for relief from
the distresses and conformities of England, and
was editing Plutarch and teaching a few pupils
advanced Greek—among them Professor Goodwin, now the veteran Greek scholar of America.
Arthur Clough had a second home at Emerson's
house in Concord, but I only met him in Cambridge. Immediately after this Concord conversation came the excitement in Boston over the
arrest of the fugitive slave Anthony Burns, and
I was present at the great meeting in Faneuil
Hall, where an unorganized attempt was made

to rescue Burns from the Court House near the City Hall, where he was confined under guard. Not being informed of the plan of rescue, I had placed myself so near the platform in the hall that it was impossible to get through the crowd to the door, and thence to Court Square, until the unsuccessful attack had been made and foiled, with one fatal wound,—that given by one of the rescuers with a sword-cane, unsheathed, to Bachelder, one of the slave's guard. As I finally got to the Court House and ran up the steps, there stood Mr. Alcott, calm and brave, his cane under his arm, ready to make another attack, if needful. It was the first time I had seen him since our philosophic *séance* in Emerson's drawing-room and study, a week before. Pressing personal duty took me the next day to Keene, whence I wrote to Emerson, May 31, to express our gratitude for his courtesies, but beginning with an acknowledgment of our mortification at being seen by his family on our walk back to Cambridge at sunset.

"We were sorry the other night to expose our

ill-fortune to you by passing your house on our
way to Lexington; but there was no other way;
it turned out, however, to be good fortune—or
I thought it so. At any rate, we could afford to
pay that price for our afternoon's enjoyment,
which we agreed was incomparable. The whole
day was to me one of the greatest delight. We
would be glad to return your hospitality by inviting you to Cambridge, to meet there a roomful
of young men, and pass the afternoon with us.
Would such an arrangement be agreeable to you,
at any time during this term? I think you told
me last year that there was an inconvenience in
it, which may still be the case. I write this from
among the Cheshire hills, not far from your Monadnoc, which I climbed our eastern hill this
morning to see. Coming here from the conten-
tion and noise of Boston, it seems like stepping
into a church—so still and cool is it here."

It must have been in response to this request,
in which Moncure Conway of Virginia, then about
graduating from the Divinity School, cordially
joined, that Emerson did visit Divinity Hall in

June, and read to a score of us in Conway's room his lecture on *Poetry*, which was not printed till many years later. It was a distinguished audience of our elder friends; for Arthur Clough came, shortly before his return to England, Longfellow and his wife were there, and Charles Lowell came with his mother, Mrs. Anna Lowell; and probably Charles Norton and William Goodwin were there, if in America, though I do not recall them. In the conversation which followed the reading, Clough took no marked part; he was extremely modest, even shy.

Many sad events for me followed these happy days of May and June: I was called away to Peterboro, New Hampshire, by the increasing illness of Miss Walker, to whom I was engaged; and this only terminated with her death in August. We were married upon her death-bed, and I remained with her aged and lonely father for a month or two, and did not return to college until October. I was invited to Concord by Emerson in November (the twenty-first), 1854, and took my first long walk with him through his Walden

woodlands, on both sides of the pond—meeting,
on our way thither, Thomas Cholmondeley, another Oxford scholar, who had followed Clough's
example, though for different reasons, and come
to spend some months in New England. He was
from New Zealand not long before, whither he
had gone to aid in the colonizing career of a relative, had raised sheep there, and written a book
about the island—*Ultima Thule* by name. Emerson introduced him to Thoreau, at whose father's
house Cholmondeley lived while in Concord, and
where he afterwards visited in 1858–59, during
the last illness of John Thoreau.

Emerson, who had dined alone that November day, was just returned from a lecture in New
Hampshire; it being his habit then, and for more
than twenty years after, to give a good part of
the autumn and winter months to lecturing in
New England, New York, Canada, and the Mid-
land States,—then called "the West,"—Ohio,
Michigan, Illinois, and finally Wisconsin, Iowa,
and Missouri—going only at intervals to New
Jersey, Pennsylvania, and at last to Washington

and Virginia, from which his pronounced anti-slavery opinions had long excluded him. In these tours he was often absent from Concord weeks or months, and encountered many interesting persons. This particular day he told me of an Illinois theorist, Bassnett by name, whom he had met, and whose book, *Outlines of a Mechanical Theory of Storms*, Emerson lent me. It proved to be totally at variance with the Newtonian system of gravitation, and, though readable from its startling theses, very slenderly supported by the facts of nature. It attached much importance to lunar influences, exerted, as Bassnett held, by means of "a vorticose motion in the luminiferous ether," which he took to be the same thing, under another name, as the electric fluid. Emerson did not accept his conclusions, but found the author entertaining, as he often thought those who break a new path in science, away from the beaten track of the professional scientist, whom he was apt to criticise humorously—as in that first chapter of what was to have been his great work on *The Natural History of Intellect*. The page was written, I suppose, before my acquaintance with him began, perhaps suggested by the controversies in which his brother-in-law, Doctor Charles T. Jackson, the famous Boston chemist and early geologist, found himself involved from time to time. Emerson there said:—

"Go into the scientific club and hearken. Each *savant* proves in his admirable discourse that he, and he only, knows now or ever did know anything on the subject. 'Does the gentleman speak of Anatomy? Who peeped into a box at the Custom House and then published a drawing of *my rat?*' Poor Nature and the sublime law are quite omitted in this triumphant vindication. Was it better when we came to the philosophers who found everybody wrong? acute and ingenious themselves to lampoon and degrade mankind."

Emerson, in all my conversations with him, as in his published writings, did not, as Harvey scoffingly said of Bacon, "talk of science like a Lord Chancellor"; but held himself modestly a listener at the shrine of Nature's oracles, and reported faithfully, without ostentation or parade, what she said in his hearing. Already, before and since his death, foremost thinkers in science and philosophy have found themselves anticipated by this subtile intelligence, musing in the woods of Concord; and little that is obsolete or obsolescent appears in the bright circle of his intellectual illumination. Ambitious systems, Positive, Cosmic, Psychical, etc., arise and vaunt themselves for a time, only to be laid aside in a few years; while the vital, spiritual philosophy of Emerson gathers strength by "years that bring the philosophic mind" to those who have been the slaves of system and a dead-and-alive logic. "Let the student," he says somewhere, "learn to appreciate this miracle of the mind. He shall come to know that in seeing, and in no tradition, he must find what truth is; shall come to trust it entirely, — to cleave to God against the name of God. When he has once known the oracle he will need no priest: He from whose hand it came will guide and direct it."

On the Saturday after this Concord walk (November 25, 1854), I dined with the Alcotts at their Pinckney Street, Boston, house, and the host, in his study afterwards, gave me this account of Emerson's method of writing, which was generally, but not absolutely, true:—

"He puts down in his common-place book from day to day, as I do in my Journal, whatever he thinks worthy; and when preparing his lectures, or writing or editing his book, he goes over these diaries, notices what topic has been uppermost in his thought for the time covered by the writing, and arranges his passages with reference to that. Does this not account for the want of formal method in his works? They are crystallizations of earlier material. We hold that a theology infused into your mind, as in Emerson's books, is better than one more directly taught. The best men, when they teach theology directly, are wont to get harsh and narrow; the indirect way is the best."

But in his style, apart from the subtler meanings, Emerson was direct enough, and did not tolerate in others what he avoided for himself. At this same date, Mr. Alcott showed me the letter of Emerson, written more than a dozen years before, criticising sincerely the language of his friend in that mystical reverie of his which he called *Psyche*, but which he never printed:—

"I think it possesses, in certain passages, the rare power to awaken the highest faculties,—to waken the apprehension of the Absolute. It is almost uniformly elegant, and contains many beautiful and some splendid pages. Its fault arises out of the subtlety and extent of its subject; it grapples with an Idea which it does not subdue and present in just method before us. The book has a strong mannerism. But its capital fault is a want of compression,—a fault almost unavoidable in treating such a subject,—which not being easily apprehensible by the human faculties, we are tempted to linger round the Idea, in the hope that what cannot be sharply stated in a few words, may yet chance to be suggested by many. . . . The prophet should speak a clear discourse, straight home to the conscience; but your page is often a series of touches. You play with the thought,—never strip off your coat, and dig and strain, and drive into the heart of the matter. See what a style yours is to balk and disappoint expectation! To use a coarse word, 't is all stir and no go. If there's a good thing, say it out! there are so few in the world, we can't wait a minute. 'Gaberdine' we have had before; say 'frock.' 'Lunch' is vulgar, and reminds one of the Bite Tavern" (in Boston).

"If there is one thing more than another," said Alcott once, "that we should pray for, it is the boon of a severely candid friend." Such did he and others find in Emerson; as those who knew him most intimately would all witness. And his censures were so friendly that, where criticism of writings was concerned, he was entitled to the praise Pope gave to the fair Belinda:—

"Who oft rejects, but never once offends."

A week after this visit to the Alcotts, I met with Emerson, Alcott, Cholmondeley, John Dwight, the musical appreciator, George Calvert, who had lived in Germany with William Emerson, and others, at an Albion dinner in Boston, and the conversation turned on literary matters and authors. Emerson was in full force, and praised and blamed with equal sincerity. He urged Mr. Dwight to print, as a publishing venture, the then new novel of *Christie Johnstone* by Charles Reade; it ought to be printed in Boston, for it was much better than *Jane Eyre*. It was soon after published by Mr. Fields, of the firm of Ticknor. George Bancroft, whose son John had lately graduated at Harvard, his father's college, was mentioned, in connection with an address he had recently given in New York, in which he lauded Calvinism, and larded his page with phrases like "Arrogant Arius," "Devout Athanasius," and the "Triune God"—Bancroft being a Unitarian, if anything, in religion. Emerson, who had first met Bancroft as a Senior in Harvard, in 1818, and who had known him well almost ever since, told us:—

"Mr. Bancroft is hardly a religious man: his Trinitarianism was perhaps assumed out of deference to the sentiment of New York, where he now lives, and which is mainly Presbyterian and

Episcopalian. In conversation he will take any
side, and defend it skilfully; he is a soldier of fortune, as we see by his political connection. His
profession of Jacksonian democracy in Boston,
where he was ostracized for it, was rewarded by
appointment to office; but Boston should have
been more tolerant of political differences. As
American minister in London he was a credit to
our country; and his speech some years earlier,
at a Phi Beta dinner in Cambridge, where Lord
Ashburton, who negotiated with Webster the
Maine Boundary treaty, was fêted, was the best
of the oratory on that occasion. The elder Quincy
and Judge Story had spoken, but rather coldly
and stiffly; but Bancroft warmed up the audience. Edward Everett was not present, having
preceded Bancroft, under Tyler's presidency, as
minister to Saint James's."

Soon after Mr. Alcott came into the Albion
dining-room, he being the oldest person present,
though only fifty-five at that time, our conversation turned on old age; and Mr. Dwight said he
could not understand why, in this earthly course

of ours, youth must be left behind. "That is, indeed, incomprehensible and sad," said Emerson; "this man here" (turning toward Alcott) "used to assure us,—what every day's experience is disproving,—that the beauty of youth turned inward." "I have the trick," he added, "of believing every man I talk with, whatever his age, to be at least as old as myself; so I warn you all, young men." The point then in question was the age of Charles Sumner, who had succeeded Daniel Webster in the Senate at Washington. As we left the Albion, I walked with Alcott and Cholmondeley to the bookstore of James Munroe on Washington Street, who had been Emerson's publisher for some years, and who had published Ellery Channing's first volumes of poems, which Cholmondeley, who had met Channing at Concord, wished to purchase and take back to Shropshire with him. Munroe himself was at the shop, and, being questioned, told us that three-fourths of all American poetry was then published at the poet's expense. This was true of Emerson's volume of 1847, and Channing's poems of the same year; his first volume, issued by Munroe in 1843, was paid for by Channing's friend, S. G. Ward. It seems that the custom of poetry-printing has not much varied since 1854; in spite of the popular success of Longfellow, Holmes, and Whittier, and finally of Lowell and Whitcomb Riley.

December 12, 1854, Mr. Alcott came out to our College to call on Morton and myself, and we went together to Morton's room in Massachusetts Hall, where we found him writing his paper on Thoreau, which I printed for him in the *Harvard Magazine* for January. This led Alcott to talk of Thoreau:—

"It is a pity that he and Emerson live in the same age; both are original, but they borrow from each other, being so near in time and space. Richard Dana says he has not read Thoreau, but always supposed him to be a man of abstractions. On the contrary, your old Librarian in the College, Doctor Harris, told me with a groan, 'If Emerson had not spoiled him, Thoreau would have made a good entomologist.'"

This same month of December, in my Senior

college year, proved to be full of serious events in my youthful life. Toward the end of it my father-in-law, worn down with age and sorrow, felt his death approaching, and I was sent for to be with him in the last hours. On my way thither (to Peterboro in New Hampshire) I passed through Boston and bade farewell to our friend Cholmondeley, who hastily decided to go home and raise a company of volunteers for the Crimean War—as he did. And it was in this month that Emerson formed the purpose of inviting me to take charge of a small school in Concord, mainly devoted to his children and those of Judge Hoar and his neighbors, in a schoolhouse built by the Judge, and not far from his father's house—Honorable Samuel Hoar's, who had married a daughter of Roger Sherman, and was, in my time, that Dantesque figure in the village streets which none could see without respect. At his death, in November, 1856, Emerson wrote his eulogy, and adorned it with a quatrain of his verse, which I have in its first form—perhaps not inferior to that which the poet afterwards printed:—

EMERSON

"With beams that stars at Christmas dart
His cold eyes truth and conduct scanned;
July was in his sunny heart,
October in his liberal hand."

Here the allusion to Christmas suggests the old-fashioned religion of this aged Christian, a true follower of Emerson's grandfather, Parson Ripley.

It was after one of his lectures in East Boston, but whether in December or January I am not certain, that Emerson proposed to me this task, or rather privilege, of educating his children and their playmates. I had gone with a few of my classmates, among whom I remember Willard Bliss, now of Rosemond, Illinois, to hear him read one chapter in his forthcoming *English Traits* to a small audience in that island ward of Boston. At the close, as we came forward to express our pleasure at the reading, he said to me, after a few words to my comrades, "Will you get into my carriage, and let me take you to the American House in Hanover Street, where I pass the night?" I accepted the favor, and, while we crossed the East Boston ferry, he unfolded to me the plan he had formed. I was to get leave of absence from college, and open the little school in March; its duties would not keep me from pursuing the Senior studies in their last three months, and I was then to continue the school after graduation, if mutually satisfactory. The salary offered, though not large, was ample for my single needs, and might be increased if the school grew in numbers, as he was kind enough to say it would, under my direction. I was to have a month or six weeks to make my decision and arrangements; and when I found that my kinsman by marriage, President Walker, then at the head of the College, would let my studies go on at Concord, I lost no time in deciding to take the place offered. Early in March, 1855, I visited the village, to call on the families of my expected pupils, and to secure rooms for myself and my sister, who, I stipulated, should be my assistant, at my own expense. Emerson escorted me on these visits; and when I asked him where I could find rooms, he said, "Mr. Ellery Channing has a large old house, with no inmates but himself and his housekeeper; we will go and see if he will take you in." We went to the house, opposite the residence of the Thoreau family; knocked, and were answered by Mr. Channing in person, wearing the oldest dressing-gown I had seen up to that time (I have since seen him come down to tea in an older one in my own house), who received us courteously, and was willing to lease me three furnished rooms, and to allow the service of his housekeeper, who was rather his tenant than his servant. That point settled, and the terms agreed on, I returned to take tea with the Emersons, and a week later began my school with seventeen pupils, girls and boys together (always the Concord custom), three of whom were Emerson's own children.

Having no previous experience with a school, though I had taught Latin and Greek pupils privately, much margin and courtesy must be allowed for my mistakes; but I received from all the families the kindest consideration, and was at home in the village and the woods from the first. One of our earliest callers was Henry Thoreau, whom I had met at Emerson's; and with his close friend, Channing, I became very intimate. I was soon introduced at the Old Manse, then occupied by that gentle scholar and excellent housekeeper Mrs. Sarah Ripley, the widow of Reverend Samuel Ripley, Emerson's half-uncle, and her daughters, all agreeable ladies, of much culture. From that acquaintance to weekly Greek readings with Mrs. Ripley was but an easy step, and thus my interest in that language was kept up. My college studies came out well; indeed, though I valued class-rank but little, I believe my "marks" were higher, from infrequent examinations, than if I had been at the daily recitations; and I graduated seventh in a class of eighty.

This is a good place to pause and speak of the scholarship of Emerson and his Concord friends. He entered Harvard at the age of fourteen, and graduated at eighteen, in 1821. In those days, and with his slender constitution, this did not imply much reading either in Latin or Greek, and French was then but little taught. In his own school-keeping, for a few years after graduation, and in his theological studies, Emerson extended

his use of Latin, and acquired both classic and
New Testament Greek so as to read it with little
difficulty; but his familiarity with the language
was never so great as Mrs. Ripley's, or (I fancy)
Miss Hoar's, who had been better taught and
more diligent in reading the originals. But from
the Attic cast of his genius, Emerson entered into
the spirit of Greek thought and literature more
profoundly than many better-equipped technical
scholars—more even than Thoreau, who was a
thorough Greek and Latin scholar. Emerson early
acquired French, both for reading and speaking, though not very fluent in conversation in
French. German he learned later, for the sole purpose of reading Goethe in the original. Italian
he read, and had some knowledge of Spanish.
Persian and Sanscrit he never attempted; but
made his translations from the German version
of Oriental authors, or such English or French
versions as were more accessible. Alcott read no
language but his own and a little French; but
Channing was versed in Latin, Greek, and all the
modern tongues of Europe, though not critically

a scholar. The same could be said of Margaret Fuller, whom I never knew.

Emerson had at all times the habit of a scholar, but one who, like Wordsworth, made the open air his library much of the time. Though not so thorough a walker and investigator of nature as his friends, Channing and Thoreau, who would spend whole days and nights in the forest or among the mountains, he had similar tastes, and in youth had much practised upon the scale they afterwards followed. When I once remarked to him that the passage in his *Woodnotes*,

> "And such I knew, a forest-seer,
> A minstrel of the natural year," *etc.*,

was generally thought to be aimed at Henry Thoreau, Emerson rather sharply negatived that notion, and told me the whole remarkable passage was conceived, largely from his own experience, and mainly written out, before he ever knew Thoreau, except as a promising boy. He was familiar with the near forests of Maine and New Hampshire, and had early seen the forest scenery of the Carolinas and Florida. In later life, when

I first knew him, his custom was to walk every day for some hours, and in these walks I was first made acquainted with several of his favorite haunts in Concord: the Walden woods, Baker Farm, Copan, and Peter's Field, leading thereto, Columbine Rock,—one of several crags thus named,—and the Estabrook country. He had composed much of his verse in these walks in field and woodland, as, indeed, the verse itself sometimes declares; and his friends were often invited to join him in his excursions, or to show him their favorite resorts. Alcott enjoyed the converse thus promoted, but hardly the walk itself; for Emerson told me, whenever they came to a farmer's fence or a convenient seat, his friend would halt, to continue their philosophic debate at rest. Alcott, at eighty-two, thus described in his *Sonnets and Canzonets* these early walks, forty years before:—

"Pleased I recall those hours so fair and free,
    When, all the long forenoons, we two did toss
    From lip to lip, in lively colloquy,
    Plato, Plotinus, or famed Schoolman's gloss,—
    Disporting in rapt thought and ecstasy;

[71]

Then by the tilting rail Millbrook we cross,
And sally through the fields to Walden wave,
There plunging in the Cove, or swimming o'er.
Through woodpaths wending, he with gesture quick
Rhymes deftly in mid-air with circling stick,
Skims the smooth pebbles from the leafy shore,
Or deeper ripples raises as we lave."

These lines well picture Emerson's habit of fore-noons in the study and afternoons in the woods, together with his manner of twirling his walking-stick, customarily carried, and his fondness for swimming in Walden, or skating there in winter. I have so skated with him, and have swum there with Alcott, when he was approaching his eigh-tieth birthday. The Concord authors, except Tho-reau, who inherited a tendency to consumption and had weakened his frame by outdoor hard-ships, were robust comrades as I knew them; for Emerson, in his first Atlantic voyage, to Sicily, in 1833, was said to have overcome his early ten-dency to phthisis, of which his brothers died. He was not expert at manual labors, as Alcott, Chan-ning, and Thoreau were, and for that reason em-ployed them occasionally in such tasks: Thoreau in his gardening and tree-planting, Channing in wood-cutting, from which experience came Channing's poem *The Woodman*, printed in his *Poems of Sixty-five Years*, and Alcott in choosing crooked sticks and making a summer house of them,—for which quaint task, satirized by Channing and Thoreau in their letters to Emerson in England, he was paid fifty dollars.

Emerson's relations with Alcott are to the lasting honor of both. Each saw the defect of the other; but Emerson, aware, as few others could be, of the profound originality of Alcott's mind and the nobility of his character, at which the worldly mocked, and even friendship sometimes wearied, never failed to stand by his friend, while dealing frankly with his foibles. He said to me, more than once, "I hope it may please the Powers to let me survive Alcott, and write his biography; for I think I can do that better than any one." It was not so ordered, and the task of biographer fell mainly to me; for Louisa Alcott died but a day or two after her father. I then reminded Doctor Emerson of what his father had told me of the records he had made of Alcott's traits and felicities, and he was good enough to copy out for me, from the diaries, most of the entries that concerned Alcott. Among them was this statement of the intrinsic manliness of character which makes the attraction of some literary men, and which Emerson, like Carlyle, recognized in Doctor Johnson:—

"The attitude is the main thing. John Bradshaw, as Milton says, was all his life a consul sitting in judgment on kings. Carlyle, best of all men in England, has kept this manly attitude in his time. His errors of opinion are as nothing in comparison with this merit, in my opinion. If I look for a counterpart in my neighborhood, Thoreau and Alcott are the best; and in majesty Alcott excels. This *aplomb* cannot be mimicked."

Had Emerson looked in his mirror, he would have seen the face of as marked an example of this quality as Alcott was—yet not so majestic in aspect, nor so graceful in manners. Our friend Cholmondeley said of Alcott, "He has the man-

ners of *a very great Peer*"—the highest compli-
ment an English Squire could pay. As Ben Jon-
son said of Bacon, "In his adversity I ever prayed
that God would give him strength, for greatness
he could not want"; so might his friends have
said of Bronson Alcott. Emerson stood ready to
aid him in every available way; yet said of him,
"With his hatred of labor and his command-
ing contemplation, a haughty beneficiary, Alcott
makes good to this nineteenth century Simeon
the Stylite, the Thebais, and the first Capuchins."
This hatred of labor was only of intellectual labor; for Alcott, like many men brought up on
ancestral acres in New England, had a real love
of manual toil, and often exhausted himself with
it in his old age, when Louisa's success had made
hand-labor needless at the Orchard House, which
Emerson had helped him purchase. Yet there was
a certain humorous truth, as often in Emerson's
compliments, in another entry in the diary about
1840, when his friend was supporting himself by
day-labor in the Concord grain-fields:—

"Alcott astonishes by the grandeur of his angle

of vision, and the heaps of particulars. I tell him he is the Bonaparte of speculators [speculative philosophers], born to rout the Austrians of the soul. But his day-labor has a certain emblematic air, like the annual plowing of the Emperor of China."

Ten years or more after my early weeks in Concord, I was present at a conversation of Alcott's which drew from Emerson these comments in his diary (1866):—

"Last night in the conversation Alcott appeared to great advantage, and I saw again, as often before, his singular superiority. As pure intellect I have never seen his equal. The people with whom he talks do not ever understand him. They interrupt him with clamorous dissent, or what they think verbal endorsement of what they fancy he may have been saying; or with 'Do you know, Mr. Alcott, I think so and so,'—some whim or sentimentalism; and do *not* know that they have interrupted his large and progressive statement; do not know that all they have in their baby brains is incoherent and spotty; that all he sees and says is like astronomy, lying there real and vast—and every part and fact in eternal connection with the whole; and that they ought to sit in silent gratitude, eager only to hear more, —to hear the whole, and not interrupt him with their prattle. His activity of mind is shown in the perpetual invention and felicity of his language; the constitutionality of his thought is apparent in the fact that last night's discourse only brought out with new conviction the fundamental thoughts which he had when I first knew him. The moral benefit of such a mind cannot be told."

To this high conception of Alcott's character and intellect Emerson was faithful to the last, and Alcott was one of the friends to whom he bade a characteristic farewell on his death-bed in 1382. Recalled for a few moments from that wandering of mind which prevailed in the last days, he grasped Alcott's hand warmly, saying, "You have a strong hold on life; be firm!" It was true, but the weight of years and the loss of his best friend weakened that hold, and it was but six months after Emerson's death that the illness of which he died six years later fell upon the vigorous frame of Alcott.

One of the first of Emerson's volumes which I read in youth was that reprint of *Nature, Addresses and Lectures* appearing in the summer of 1849, and directly followed by *Representative Men* later in the year. While these books were going through the press in Boston, Alcott had frequent colloquies with Emerson on their theories of "Genesis" (as Alcott styled what is now termed Evolution), and one of the most distinct expressions of the evolutionary theory was handed by Emerson to Alcott in August, 1849,—who pasted into his diary the remarkable verse, about to be used as the new motto for *Nature:*—

> "A subtle chain of countless rings
> The next unto the farthest brings;
> The eye reads omens where it goes,
> And speaks all languages the Rose;
> And, striving to be man, the worm
> Mounts through all the spires of form."

How much earlier this was written is yet unknown; but it was the conclusion to which Emerson had been coming for a dozen years, helped by the discoveries and theories of Oken, Goethe, and Swedenborg. In 1855, when I was one day with Emerson in his study, he read me these lines, and asked me how I should interpret them:—

"Caught among the blackberry vines,
 Feeding on the Ethiops sweet,
 Pleasant fancies overtook me.
 I said, 'What influence me preferred,
 Elect, to dreams thus beautiful?'
 The vines replied, 'And did'st thou deem
 No wisdom to our berries went?'"

I hardly knew what to reply, where several meanings were possible; but said that he must have meant that Nature does not leave her least particle without a lesson for Man; that the moral of the delicious flavor of the low blackberry was, "Even so, what seems black to you in Man's destiny may have as fair an issue; as Cowper says:—

"The bud may have a bitter taste,
 But sweet will be the flower."

Without commenting on this, it seemed to please him; and I inferred it was an illustration of his philosophic principle:—

"The eye reads omens where it goes."

It may have been this incident that determined me, the next year, to set my advanced class of girls reading Emerson's *Poems* of 1847, then but little known, and commenting on them myself, by way of interpretation. This was, so far as I know, the first example of what has since become a frequent practice, in which my friend Charles Malloy of Waltham is a past master; he being an older Emersonian than myself. Emerson seldom commented his own verses, except by way of correction of a mistaken reading; and, like all poets, he did not always know which the best word was. Thus, when he read me that fine group of poems which, at much urgency on their part, he gave to the beginners of *The Atlantic Monthly* for their first number, the best of them all, *Days*, began:—

"*Daughters* of Time, the hypocritic Days;"

and so he printed it in *The Atlantic*, a year afterwards. But when he afterwards printed it, the beginning shocked me with its

"*Damsels* of Time."

Now "damsels" is a good word in some connections, but not in a grave, finished Greek epigram, which this poem is; just as Thoreau's *Smoke* is, —graceful as Meleager, and profound as Simonides. The better reading is now restored in the posthumous volume of *Poems*. But omissions occurred there which I cannot quite understand. In that strangely admirable *Woodnotes* a slight change is made in the lines,

> "He shall *see* the speeding year
> Without wailing, without fear,"

by altering "see" to "meet"—perhaps to make it less apparently a version (a much improved one) of those lines of Horace which Emerson once told me were the grandest of that smiling poet:—

> " *Hunc solem et stellas et decedentia certis*
> *Tempora momentis, sunt qui, formidine nulla*
> *Imbuti, spectent.*"
>
> (Epistle VI. To Numicius.)

Horace gave us the majestic Lucretian rhythm, and, like Dante, introduced the stars effectively; but the pith of the passage is in Emerson's short couplet. It might be rendered without so much compression:—

"Yon Sun and Stars, and fatal flight of days,—
There are, my Friend, who view with fearless gaze."

But the Greeks would have shortened the expression as Emerson did. In the same *Woodnotes* describing the same "coming man,"

"Whom Nature giveth for defence
His formidable innocence,"

this hyperbole is omitted, perhaps wisely, where so much is hyperbole:—

"He shall never be old,
Nor his fate shall be foretold."

But why leave out this magical sketch of the sorceress?

"The robe of silk in which she shines,
It was woven of many sins;
And the shreds which she sheds
In the wearing of the same,
Shall be grief on grief and shame on shame."

There is an imperfect rhyme, to be sure, and the thought is incoherent—but so is the creature depicted; and like to like is good, to say nothing of the pleasing rhythm.

I have mentioned hyperbole. It was Emerson's most familiar trope and prevailed in his speeches and his daily conversation. In fact, Concord might be styled the land of Hyperbole and Humor,— so abundant are they in the writings of all the famous authors there, except Hawthorne, who substituted a rhetorical vitascope. In the summer of 1856 I was mostly engaged in visiting Middlesex towns, holding meetings, and raising money to keep Kansas free from negro slavery. Our college tutor in elocution, Mr. Jennison, for a Cambridge committee, arranged a meeting in Lyceum Hall, opposite the Colleges (September 10, 1856), at which Emerson consented to speak, so much was he concerned for our national political situation. In his speech, which I heard, he introduced a passage, not set down in his notes, and which does not appear in the printed report. Speaking of the anti-slavery opinions of the founders of the Republic (Washington, Jefferson, Franklin, Madison), and the absence of such men from the ranks of the conspirators against liberty to-day, he quoted the antithesis of Tacitus, remarking on the absence of the busts of Brutus and Cassius from the funeral procession of Junia, who was

wife of Cassius and sister of Brutus: "Sed præ-
fulgebant Cassius atque Brutus, eo ipso, quod
effigies eorum non visebantur,"—"Eo ipso præ-
fulgebant," cried Emerson, "quod non visebantur!
Yes, *they glared out of their absence.*" Here was
hyperbole again, and compression of the already
concise Roman annalist.

In conversation it was the same. I was taking
tea one evening at the Emersons' before the Civil War, when Mrs. Emerson, just returned from
Boston, where some of her friends were ardent
Episcopalians, had been ruffled by the spiritual
pride of some dignitary of Henry the Eighth's
church, whose quoted remark implied there was
no true religion anywhere in New England out-
side of what he styled "The Church," with a
capital C. She was telling us what her reply had
been to the lady quoting the dictum. "And did
you tell her, Queenie" (Emerson's domestic title
for his wife), "that it is the church of all the
donkeys in America?" with his most benevolent
smile. Now he did not mean that all that class
of our people were Anglicans,—only to satirize a

sect which at that time had not its fair share of the ideas and scientific truth of the American people; but was still apt to think that geology was an atheistic attack on Moses and the Book of Genesis.

Without being a partisan in his turn of mind, as the brothers Hoar of Concord were, Emerson was frank and direct in his advocacy of what he thought the national cause at any time; and this made him earnest in behalf of Charles Sumner and the exclusion of slavery from Kansas. He spoke warmly at the meeting in Concord Town Hall (where he must have read lectures or made speeches fifty times from 1852 till his death, thirty years later) to protest against the assault on Massachusetts through her senator, when he was almost assassinated by Brooks of Carolina. And when, a few days later, our first Kansas meeting was held there, resulting in a general subscription of money to aid the Free-State men in Kansas, Emerson was one of the large givers. As secretary of the meeting, I retained the subscription paper, and some of the names may be mentioned.

Concord was then a town of less than half its present population,—not twenty-three hundred in 1855,—and contained few persons of wealth, the largest property not exceeding two hundred and fifty thousand dollars probably. Yet the first subscription for Kansas was nearly one thousand dollars, and there were four givers of one hundred dollars each: Samuel Hoar, and his son Judge Hoar, John S. Keyes, and F. B. Sanborn. Four gave fifty dollars each: R. W. Emerson, Colonel Whiting, Nathan Brooks (father-in-law of Judge Hoar), and Ozias Morse; six gave twenty-five dollars each: George M. Brooks, Samuel Staples, John Brown, Jr., Daniel B. Clarke, Reuben Rice, and "A Lady"—probably either Mrs. Emerson or Miss Hoar; then followed subscriptions of twenty, ten, and five dollars; while a few children and poor men gave from fifty cents to two dollars each. These subscriptions were afterwards increased by gifts of money, clothing, etc., until before a year passed they had amounted to nearly or quite two thousand dollars—or almost a dollar each for every inhabitant. When in the summer following I became a member and secretary of the State Kansas Committee, and in that capacity visited the National Committee's office in Chicago, and then went further west, to call on the Governor of Iowa, and traverse that State as far as to Nebraska City on the west of the Missouri River, I corresponded with Emerson. The next winter, he made the acquaintance of John Brown, the Kansas hero, who had come to visit me in Concord, and Emerson invited him to his house for a night. In this visit was acquired that full knowledge of Brown's character (though not of his secret plans) which enabled Emerson at the time of the Virginia foray and capture of Brown, to tell his story effectively before large audiences in Boston and Salem. Mr. Alcott, in 1878, gave me this account of Emerson's and Thoreau's reception of the news of the Harper's Ferry affair.

"When the tidings came that John Brown was captured, I was with Henry Thoreau at Emerson's house. It was startling to all of us. Thoreau spoke of it then much as he soon afterwards did publicly—addressing his townsmen in the parish vestry, and the people of Worcester and Boston, with his *Plea for Captain John Brown*. [Mr. Alcott thought Thoreau rang the bell himself for this Concord address, but he probably confounded the occasion with that in August, 1844, when Emerson was to give his address on *West India Emancipation*, mentioned earlier in this book. At that time Thoreau not only rang the bell, but previously had gone about the village, giving notice at the house-doors that Emerson would speak at the vestry.] I said that Brown's death would be a new crucifixion, and dwelt upon the fact of Brown's martyrdom. Emerson said little then; it seemed to be a painful subject to him. Some weeks after, when he had returned from Salem, where he made that much-quoted speech in praise of Brown (of which he gave you the manuscript), he said to me, with an air of relief, 'We have had enough of this dreary business.' But when we were making arrangements, with Thoreau and yourself and others, for that 'Service for the Death of a Martyr' which we held at the Concord Town Hall, the day of Brown's execution, Emerson made some of the best selections used, and read them himself at the meeting, as Thoreau did his selections from Marvell and Tacitus."

In truth, as Hazlitt says of Sir Francis Burdett, there was no honest cause Emerson dared not avow, no oppressed person whom he was not forward to succor. He did not wholly agree with the Garrisonian Abolitionists, but he supported their main cause, as he did Brown's.

It was during my first residence in Concord, and while Hawthorne was our consular representative at Liverpool, that I became acquainted through Emerson with the theories and caprices of Miss Delia Bacon, of New Haven, who may be said to have invented, as much as any one person did, that craze now grown to such magnitude, — that Bacon of Saint Albans wrote the plays and poems of Shakespeare. This was not exactly Miss Bacon's first whim, but that the plays came as the product of a circle of great men of Elizabeth's court, — Raleigh, Bacon, and others; a theory that finds some countenance, though very slight, in John Toland's odd letter of two centuries ago declaring that there was such a circle, and that Giordano Bruno, then in England, belonged to it in 1585. Bruno dedicated one of his quaint books to Sidney, whom Toland thought one of the company; and there are certain faint indications that Shakespeare had read and understood Bruno's ideas. Miss Bacon, a brilliant, unhappy person, came to Emerson with her theory in 1852; he listened to her with patience and interest, though not persuaded. When she was aided by a citizen of New York to pursue her inquiries in England, Emerson gave her letters to Carlyle, Doctor Chapman, and other English friends, and in her destitution he commended her to Hawthorne at Liverpool. He procured for her first essays on the subject a publisher in America, as Carlyle did in London. *Putnam's Magazine*, then flourishing, and having among its contributors Henry James, G. W. Curtis, and (rarely) Thoreau and Emerson himself, accepted an article or two from Miss Bacon. One such appeared there; another, in a manuscript or half-printed state, was lost on the way from New York to Concord, intrusted to a relative of Emerson. This loss, later, led to reproaches from Miss Bacon which Emerson did not wholly escape. Her proud and whimsical character, verging toward insanity, made these favors from her friends useless to her; and when she turned upon him (as later upon Hawthorne) with these reproaches, Emerson's angelic patience did not resent it. Finally, her insanity declared itself without disguise, and she was committed to an asylum not far from Shakespeare's grave. It fell to Emerson to communicate this dismal fact to her brother, Reverend Doctor Bacon of New Haven, who had been less tolerant of her infirmities than the Concord authors had. Here is his noble letter:—

"CONCORD, February 18, 1858.

"DEAR SIR:

"*I have received from Mrs. Flower, of Stratford-on-Avon, the en-*
"*closed note, which I hasten to forward to you. I could heartily*
"*wish that I had very different news to send you of a person who*
"*has high claims on me, and all of us who love genius and elevation*
"*of character. These qualities have so shone in Miss Bacon that,*

[91]

" while their present eclipse is the greater calamity, it seems as if the
" care of her in these present distressing circumstances ought not to
" be at private, but at the public charge of scholars and friends of
" learning and truth. If I can serve you in any manner in relation
" to her, you will please to command me.

" With great respect,
" R. W. EMERSON.

" DR. LEONARD BACON.*"*

"Osman," said Emerson, sketching himself, whether consciously or not, "had a humanity so broad and deep that, although his speech was so bold and free with the Koran as to disgust all the dervishes, yet there was never a poor outcast, eccentric or insane man,—some fool who had cut off his beard, or who had been mutilated under a vow, or had a pet madness in his brain,—but fled at once to him. That great heart lay there so sunny and hospitable in the centre of the country that it seemed as if the instinct of all sufferers drew them to his side. And the madness which he harbored he did not share."

Instances confirmatory of this might be multiplied. The milder eccentricities of genius, seen in his friends Alcott, Thoreau, and Channing, were of course more easily borne with, and were only spoken of by Emerson for instruction to a younger friend, or for a harmless smile. He told his daughter Ellen that if he should die before Alcott and Channing "two good books will be lost." He formed the acquaintance with the three in the order followed above,—Alcott first and Channing third. Mr. Alcott told me in 1878, after we had bathed together in Walden, one hot August day, that he first heard Emerson preach in Doctor Channing's church in Federal Street, Boston, in 1829, on *The Universality of the Moral Sentiment.* "I was greatly struck with the youth of the preacher, the beauty of his elocution, and the direct, sincere manner in which he addressed his hearers. But I did not become acquainted with the young clergyman till after my return from Philadelphia (where Anna and Louisa were born) in 1834, when I established my Temple School in Boston. We became intimate, and soon after, I went with Emerson to hear him read a Phi Beta poem at Harvard College, in which was a striking passage about Washington. As the procession was forming to enter the church where the oration and poem were to be given, Emerson took my arm (I not being a member of the Society, nor even a graduate of Yale) and saying, 'Come, we will not mince matters,' stepped briskly along with me at his side into the church. When his time came to read the poem from the platform, Emerson read smoothly for a while; then, not feeling satisfied with what he had written, closed his reading abruptly and sat down."

The next day, as I was sitting with Emerson to entertain him while Wyatt Eaton was sketching his portrait for *Scribner's Magazine*, I asked him about this poem. He said he had composed such a poem, and it may have had a passage in it about Washington; but he had quite forgotten the facts about its delivery in Cambridge. After his father's death, Doctor Emerson told me that this poem was written for delivery in 1834; that it contained two striking passages, one on Washington and another on Lafayette, besides the lines on Webster which are printed among the posthumous poems (edition of 1884). The whole poem is in the measure of Pope and Dryden, with an occasional Alexandrine; and I fancy that the remarkable lines in *Woodnotes* beginning

"In unplowed Maine he sought the lumberers' gang,"

were intended for this poem, which has never been printed entire. Channing entered Harvard this year (1834) and Thoreau had entered the year before.

At various dates from 1860 to 1880, Emerson spoke to me of Thoreau, saying, among other things: "He was a person who said and wrote surprising things, not accounted for by anything in his antecedents,—his birth, his education, or his way of life. But why is he never frank? That was an excellent saying of Elizabeth Hoar's about him: 'I love Henry, but I can never like him.' What is so cheap as politeness? I have no social pleasure with Henry, though more than once the best conversation. Yes, I know he needs cherishing and care. Yet who can care and cherish, when we are so driven with our own affairs? Longfellow and Lowell have not appreciated Thoreau as a thinker and writer, and Judge Hoar has confirmed them in their scepticism. Henry makes an instant impression, one way or the other. He met Thomas Cholmondeley in my house, in 1854,—you also met that singularly verdant Englishman there, —who was so pleased with the nonchalant manner of Thoreau that he went at once and engaged to board at Mrs. Thoreau's, where his admiration of Henry grew greater by daily contact. Thoreau did not at first appreciate his Shropshire friend, but came to value him highly."

In 1874–75, Emerson was much in favor of printing Thoreau's journals entire, particularly the natural history in them. He said that he advised Miss Thoreau (who died in 1876) to put the journals in my charge, as they had been for a time, while I was living in her house, where the manuscripts remained for many years after Thoreau's death. He told her that I could well select the passages for printing, and could call on Mr. Channing to aid in editing them, as she had done, soon after Henry's death. The mention of Channing displeased her; she told Emerson that, without asking her consent, or giving her knowledge of what he was to do with them, Channing had gone to Henry's room in the west attic, taken the journals, or some of them, and kept them for a time. Fearing that he would have access to them in my custody, she had requested Emerson to have them removed to the town library. At her death she left them to Mr. Blake. Emerson regretted this; he had read the selections made by Mr. Blake and printed in *The Atlantic*, and did not think the best selections had been made, or the best arrangement followed. He said he read Channing's *Thoreau, the Poet-Naturalist* when it came out in 1873, but did not wholly like it; he would read it again, since I praised it.[2]

When Emerson's edition of Thoreau's Letters and a few poems came out, I remonstrated with him for printing so few of the verses. He replied that he had chosen the best, and that it would do Thoreau no credit to print them all, as I suggested,—every line, whether good or bad, as we do with the verse of the Greeks, whom Thoreau in some points so resembled. He remained firm in his view, and afterwards told me (in 1878) that Thoreau's best poem was the earliest one, *Sympathy*, published first in *The Dial* in 1840.

In his early relations with Alcott in Concord (1840–41), there were incidents that have escaped notice, I think. Soon after the Alcott family reached Concord, spending the first night at the Middlesex tavern, Mr. Emerson was summoned there to perform the wedding ceremony for the landlord's daughter, Miss Wesson, who married Sam Staples, then an assistant in the tavern, but afterwards deputy sheriff and jailer; and at this ceremony Mr. Alcott was a witness. At Mr. Emerson's own Plymouth wedding in 1835, Sam, as the stable boy, had taken to him at the Old Manse the horse and chaise which was to convey the bridegroom to Miss Jackson's Winslow Mansion for the ceremony. He was then living with his mother at Doctor Ripley's, and was paying for the board of both the sum of eight dollars only a week — with a stipulation that when both were at home, they should have a fire together in one of the parlors, and when Mr. Emerson was absent,

his mother should have a fire in her own chamber.
Considering that he was thus the more expensive
of the two, he proposed to his grandfather that he
should pay five dollars of the eight, and his mother but three. In 1841, before the Alcotts had
been in Concord a year, Emerson proposed, with
the approval of his wife, that Mr. Alcott and his
family (a wife and four children) should occupy
"half our house and store-room free"; Mr. Alcott
to work in the garden, and Mrs. Alcott to share
the household labors with Mrs. Emerson. The
families and tables were to be separate, "save one
oven to bake our puddings and the same pot for
our potatoes; but not the same cradle for our
babies." Mrs. Alcott had the practical good sense
to decline this generous but embarrassing offer;
which was as near as Emerson ever came, I think,
to the project of a community for himself.

It was a little earlier than this that Emerson
had formed his friendship with the shy and capri-
cious poet Ellery Channing. They were brought
together in Boston, in December, 1840, by the
good offices of Samuel Gray Ward of Boston

(now of Washington), who had for some years
shared with Miss Caroline Sturgis of Boston the
hazardous position of Channing's intimate. Emerson, who had seen some of his early verses, and
even printed them in the October *Dial,* had long
been eager to meet the poet; but he was either
on the prairies of Illinois, or on the road to or
from the West, or shunning society in Boston, or
at Curzon's Mill, or at "Aunt Becky Atkins's" in
Newburyport. Finally they came together, these
two poets, and each enjoyed the other. Their
correspondence, fitful and moody on Channing's
part, brief and wise from Emerson's pen, displays
a singular friendship, extending over more than
forty years, and, so far as Emerson is concerned,
justifying his sweet verse in the *Essays:*—

> "I fancied he was fled,
>   And, after many a year,
>   Glowed unexhausted kindliness
>   Like daily sunrise there."

On Channing's part the conditions vary greatly.
He never loses his admiration for Emerson's
genius, nor quite fails in gratitude for the con-

stant services which Emerson renders; but the moods of a disappointed man are hard to restrain. That remoteness and aloofness of Emerson at times, of which I spoke early in this book, gave Channing real agony; he was formed for the closest intimacy with a very few persons, he had fixed his affection upon Emerson, and it did not seem to him to be returned. "Unappreciated! It is this," he said, in a letter to another friend, "which strikes through the soul of a man like a slow fire. It is no longer Nature; persons begin to assume a terrific value to me. I thought I had done with persons. No—they rise and tear me, year after year." But this is only one of the phases of this long friendship. At other times, and for the most part, there was cordiality in Emerson, and a nearer approach to sympathy than with a somewhat socially rude nature, such as Thoreau's was, in contrast with Emerson's centuries of social culture.

Channing's special gift was æsthetic; he could take his friends, and he often took Emerson, to scenes in the landscape which opened new ideas in art, and new views of Nature. In literature, too, as in art, his scope was wide and his judgment manly and delicate. His humor was suffusing and irresistible; the wretchedness of which he so often spoke, and which indeed haunted him, was soothed and often dispelled by his love of Victor Cousin's trinity: the Good, the Beautiful, and the True. These abstractions, as with Shakespeare and Homer, floated in a sea of humor, softly lapsing or noisily mirthful,—the *anerithmon gelasma* of a Greek poet. To Emerson, whose study was Man and Nature, and whose life craved variety, Channing furnished that element of the unexpected which is so apt to be lost in a long friendship, and perhaps was finally lost in this one.

Thus, about 1878, when I was relating to Emerson what constant topics of enlivening conversation Channing brought with him to his walks and talks with me, Emerson sighed and said, "It used to be so with me, but of late he says little or nothing, and I do not find in him that 'inexhaustible fund of good fellowship' of which Thoreau told Ricketson, and which was once in him." Probably there was a fault on both sides,

—a little lack of confidence on Emerson's part, after Channing had printed, without consulting him, some passages copied with his consent from Emerson's journals, years before; and on Channing's part some grief at this withdrawal. Thoreau, in a similar experience, had confided to his journal the suffering he felt, but Channing, who kept journals but semi-occasionally, had no such resource. His letters to Emerson which are preserved, and may some time be published, contain many passages showing deep insight and frequent grace of expression. During his short residence in New York in 1844–45, he thus described his way of letter-writing, and his preference for the country over the city (December 19, 1844):—

"Would to God I had something to tell you worth your hearing! Don't thank me in any of your letters for mine. When I am at home I run into your house; when I am away I run in by means of a letter. Do not look upon it in any other light, for Heaven's sake. I have no idea of being estranged at all from your house by coming a few paltry hundred miles and taking up my quarters here. I fear I shall have a barren winter in New York. I do not require the city; it is no tug on my faculties. It does tug me to live in the country,—in the hard, still, severe, iron-bound fields of New England. There, in solitude, I paced many a day, treading wearily the lone avenues of the silent woods, sustained only in life by the breath of the sky. To dwell there is sufficient to test and reduce all the powers of a man,—a solitary, severe life, a time of wailing and barrenness. There is not a field in that village but I have watered it with my tears."

Few of Emerson's letters have been published; many of them should be. Those which appear in these pages will indicate what treasures they contain. That which I am now to give illustrates his constant generosity toward other authors, and his high appreciation of this poet of whom we have been hearing. It relates to the incomplete manuscript of Channing's "colloquial poem," as he quaintly called it, *The Wanderer*, which had been in my hands some months when I submitted it to Emerson, a year before it was printed by Os-

Concord—
13 November, 1870

My dear Sir,

I ought not
to have returned the MSS.
You were so good & careful
to lend me, without special
acknowledgment. But on the
day when I received your
note, I was busy with work
which I was to carry in
the morning to Boston to be
more busy there in finishing
the same. Indeed, I have
been such a hack lately
with my things, &, as it
happened, a sick hack
too, that I have not done

justice to that Manuscript in all this time. Yet I read the two first parts not only with great pleasure, but with surprise at the power & the fidelity of the writing. When you can see through the handwriting, the thought is so active & original, the observation of nature so incessant, that it must be attractive, I think, to all good readers. It absolves the writer instantly from the charge of idleness or solitariness, by showing that his immense vacation is all well spent. What botany & ornithology & wonderful eye for landscape, he has. I long to see & read it all in fair print. The third part "the Sea", I did not finish, perhaps did not read far:— it seemed to me not nearly so happily written, & being, as I have said, myself preoccupied, did not return to it. I could not resist the showing "Monadnoc" to Ellen & Edward, who read it with real joy. I heartily hope that the book can & will be printed, as it will, I think, conquer to itself available public, & thereby essentially benefit the author in more ways than a good sale. With great regard, yours,

F. B. Sanborn, Esq.   R. W. Emerson

good in Boston. He returned it to me, after some weeks, with this letter, sent to Springfield, where I was living from 1868 to 1872, in which year I returned to Concord.

"CONCORD, 13 November, 1870.

"MY DEAR SIR:

"I ought not to have returned the Manuscript you were so good and "careful to lend me, without special acknowledgment. But on the "day when I received your note, I was busy with work which I was "to carry in the morning to Boston, to be more busy there in fin- "ishing the same. Indeed, I have been such a hack lately with my "things, and as it happened, a sick hack, too, that I have not done "justice to that Manuscript in all this time.

"Yet I read the two first parts not only with great pleasure, but "with surprise at the power and the fidelity of the writing. When "you can see through the handwriting, the thought is so active and "original, the observation of nature so incessant, that it must be "attractive, I think, to all good readers. It absolves the writer in- "stantly from the charge of idleness or solitariness, by showing that "his immense vacation is all well spent. What botany and orni- "thology and wonderful eye for landscape he has! I long to see "and read it all in fair print.

"The third part, the 'Sea' I did not finish,—perhaps did not "read far,—it seemed to me not nearly so happily written; and "being, as I have said, myself preoccupied, I did not return to it. "I could not resist the showing 'Monadnoc' to Ellen and Edward, "who read it with loud joy. I heartily hope that the book can and

[105]

" will be printed, as it will, I think, conquer to itself a valuable pub-
" lic, and thereby essentially benefit the author in more ways than a
" good sale.

> *" With great regard yours,*
>> *" R. W. EMERSON.*

" F. B. SANBORN, ESQ."

The Emerson children here mentioned as reading the descriptions of "Cheshire's haughty hill,"
as Emerson styled his favorite mountain in the
Concord prospect, had themselves spent days and
nights on Monadnoc with Channing and their
younger friends; and a part of the poem dealt
with them and their adventures there. The pleasure they took in the reading had one inconvenience for me. They could not refrain from quoting some of his own verses to the author, when
taking tea at the Emerson house, and this re-
vealed to the quick-witted poet that his manuscript, which he had intrusted to me to find him
a publisher, had been in Emerson's hands, to
whom he had not himself intended to show it till
it should appear "in fair print." He therefore instantly wrote to me in Springfield, asking the
return of the sheets. I had got a part of them

copied, but not all, and I replied that I would bring them with me to Concord at an early date, when the copy was completed; and this I did, without explaining to him what use Emerson had made of the first part of the poem. Afterwards, when we had found a publisher, it was agreed that Emerson should write a preface, as he did —using some of the same expressions found in the above letter.

During their long familiarity Ellery Channing noted down a few of the remarks which Emerson made in a thousand conversations, and Emerson did the like by Channing. Some of these appear in the chapters of Channing's *Thoreau* which he called "Walks and Talks" and "Characters"; others will be given here. Some of Emerson's comments came out in *The Atlantic Monthly* last July (1902), but with misprints that injured their effect. The passage dated in 1859, for instance, where it relates to Channing's poem of *Near Home*, printed in 1858, should read thus:—

"Channing, who writes a poem for our fields, begins to help us. That is construction, and better than running to Charlemagne and Alfred for subjects. *Near Home* is a poem which would delight the heart of Wordsworth, though genuinely original, and with a simplicity of plan which allows the writer to leave out all the prose. 'T is a series of sketches of natural objects such as abound in New England, enwreathed by the thoughts they suggest to a contemplative pilgrim,—

'Unsleeping truths by which wheels on Heaven's prime.'

There is a neglect of superficial correctness which looks a little studied, as if perhaps the poet challenged notice to his subtler melody; and strokes of skill which recall the great masters. There is nothing conventional in the thought or the illustration; but

'Thoughts that voluntary move
Harmonious numbers'

and pictures seen by an instructed eye."

In his mention of "two notable acquaintances of mine, not else to be approximated," Emerson had in mind, I suppose, Henry Thoreau and William Tappan, in whose acquaintance "W. E. C.

served as a companion of H. D. T., and Tappan
of Channing." This, at any rate, is what occurred.
Again, in the earliest mention of Channing in
these *Atlantic* passages, the date should be 1840,
not 1841, and the remark, "C.'s eyes are a com-
pliment to the human race," etc., was meant to
apply to Caroline Sturgis, to whom and of whom
Channing wrote some of his best early poems. On
this point Emerson said to me in 1874, and sub-
sequently: "Ellery Channing's earliest friends
were Caroline Sturgis and S. G. Ward, by whom
he was introduced to me in 1840, after I had
printed some of his verses in *The Dial* as 'New
Poetry.' You know his father, Doctor Walter
Channing; his uncle, Doctor Channing the minister, was the patron of my early studies in divinity. He was one of three persons whom I have
heard speak more eloquently than any others; and
I never could find in the hymns what I heard
Doctor Channing read from them in his high
pulpit. Ellery's mother dying early [in 1822,
while Doctor Channing was in England]. he was
brought up for a while by his mother's aunt, Mrs.

Bennett Forbes, sister of Colonel T. H. Perkins, who lived at Milton and was the mother of our friend, John Murray Forbes. Mrs. William Hunt [wife of the painter], who was herself a Perkins, ascribes all Ellery's peculiarities to the Perkins blood, of which she tells sad stories. His father, Doctor Walter Channing, went abroad for his medical education; when he went again in our time, and, returning from Russia, came here to Concord to see his son, he found Ellery just starting out for an afternoon walk. He did not give it up for the sake of seeing his father, but left him in the house where you once lived, to entertain himself as he might with his grandchildren. I have seldom heard Ellery speak of Mr. Alcott otherwise than as a fool; yet he has written me some of the best things in praise of Alcott. I do not remember hearing of *Major Leviticus*, a long prose sketch, in which Alcott is satirized; but I now have in my possession a thick prose manuscript which Channing brought me many years ago, but which I did not think good enough to print, and in which probably Alcott is mentioned. Ellery began by being very intimate with Miss Elizabeth Hoar; then suddenly broke off the acquaintance, and would not look at her when he met her in the street; but he has recently [1874] renewed his intimacy with her."

In this conversation, among others, Emerson said to me "I hope it will please Mr. Alcott to die first, so that I can write his biography." He added: "I formerly and usually took the greatest pleasure in his conversation. It is no longer so, but I suppose that is my own fault. I am in the habit of saying that he cannot write; but he has this gift of conversation, and the most distinguished manners. Of this I have seen surprising instances at his conversations, in meeting the annoyances of unappreciative interrupters; Alcott parrying their frivolous questions with great wit and delicacy of tact." In 1878, when Emerson was asked to send verses to be printed anonymously in *A Masque of Poets*, which Roberts was soon to publish, I told him that Mr. Alcott had some verses there, and that he had before printed several poems; to which he replied, "Mr. Alcott is a brilliant talker, but he cannot write anything; I should know he could never write a line of verse." It was in this conversation that Emerson assured me it was settled that he could not himself write poetry; and a few moments after he added, "Others have found this out at last, but I could have told them so long ago." His daughter whispered that he had taken this idea from something Carlyle had said about John Sterling, whom he would not allow to be a poet, though he had written some fine verses. It was soon after this that Alcott began to compose those *Sonnets and Canzonets* published in 1882, just before Emerson's death, which disprove the absolute negative of this friend on his power of writing verse; for these octogenarian sonnets have a peculiar merit, not often found in portrait-sketches in metrical form. The earliest of the poems in this book came to my notice under affecting circumstances, as this entry from my journal shows:—

(*Sunday, January 4, 1880.*) "At half-past three to-day, Mr. Alcott called at my house by the river, to spend the afternoon, and read me some 'notes' as he said. These proved to be the stanzas of a new poem on the death of his daughter May (Madame Nieriker, the wife of Ernst Nieriker of Baden in Switzerland, temporarily residing in Paris), who died near Paris, on December 30, 1879. She had been absent from Concord for nearly three years, and was married in London a year ago. The poem he calls *Love's Morrow* and it has been written in the nights and mornings since he had tidings of this youngest daughter's death, on the last day of the old year. He was himself eighty years old on the twenty-ninth of November last; his daughter Louisa forty-seven on the same day, and May thirty-nine years old last July. It seemed to me the finest of Mr. Alcott's many poems which I have seen; expressing with simplicity and pathos the grief he now feels. He desired me to counsel him as to the form in certain lines, and the use of particular words; some of these, at his suggestion or mine, were changed. He spoke touchingly and with discrimination of May; saying that he felt her loss more than that of his wife two years before. 'There was

[113]

an earthly future for May, with her child, but none for Mrs. Alcott at her age' (seventy-seven). As I was making for him a copy of the poem, with the changes, Mr. Emerson, who had called at Mr. Alcott's house near by, to sympathize with him in his bereavement, finding he was with me, came over, and they had a long conversation by themselves.

"It was now five o'clock and more, and, after some urging, he stayed to tea, and with him his daughter Ellen, who had called to escort him home, at the other end of the village. Mr. Alcott also stayed, and the conversation soon became general, and reminiscent, as it often is with Emerson of late years. He said that a classmate of his brother William, John Everett, a younger brother of Edward and Alexander Everett, was a superior person, with as much genius as Edward, and of a more imposing appearance. He was noted in College, as Edward had been, for eloquence in declamation, 'and I remember exactly how he uttered Byron's lines in *Childe Harold*, which we all knew by heart then:—

"Three hosts combine to offer sacrifice,
  Three tongues prefer strange orisons on high,
  Three gaudy standards flout the pale blue skies;
  The shouts are France! Spain! Albion! Victory!
  The foe, the victim, and the fond ally," *etc.*

When Byron had nothing to say, which was often, he yet said it magnificently. John Everett's address to his classmates, on graduating, was printed at the time, and is a very good piece of writing. Edward Hale, his nephew, has lately sent me a copy, and I read it, after many years, with new pleasure. He became a tutor in the Transylvania University in Kentucky; but in a visit to Boston in 1826, after speaking eloquently in Faneuil Hall, he went home to a house where Miss Ellen Tucker was then living, and she heard him fall dead in a room over hers.

"'William Emerson, after graduating and teaching a school in Boston, went to Germany to complete his studies for the ministry; but had his opinions so much modified by what he learned there that he had doubts of his fitness for the pulpit. He went to see Goethe at Weimar, to ask his advice about preaching, and the old poet urged him to conform to custom and preach in spite of his doubts. My brother could not do that; he returned to Boston and came to see me in Chelmsford, where I had a school,—telling me that "he could not be a minister." I was very sad, for I knew how much it would grieve my mother, as it did. We were all ministers for generations. She was a lady of the old stock, my mother,—had been a member of Doctor Gardiner's Episcopal Church in Boston, and was converted to Unitarianism by her husband, my father. Aunt Mary Emerson was a genius and a great writer.

"'Afterwards, when I was studying for the ministry at Divinity Hall in Cambridge, Professor Andrews Norton was lecturing there; and he allowed me, who for a year could use my eyes but little, to hear the lectures without being examined on the subjects. If they had examined me, they would perhaps not have let me preach at all. Professor Norton was then a scholastic person, who had the air of living among his books at Shady Hill, near the College; he was not a man of society, as I think. Edward Everett, a younger scholar, who had studied in Germany, was admired by all the young men when he taught Greek at Cambridge; we were sorry when he went into political life, and was sent to Congress, for which he was not fitted. Alexander Everett seemed to me a heavy person; his brothers had genius, but he had only talent.'"

At this date, little more than two years before his death, Emerson seldom took part any longer in public conversations, being distrustful of his memory; which, however, was good for remote events, such as those above mentioned. He often spoke of his college days, and on one occasion related to Elizabeth Peabody, in the presence of his brother Charles, an incident of his intercourse with the professor of rhetoric, Edward Channing, a brother of the preacher, who had a great name for improving the style of his pupils. Emerson had written a poem for a college exhibition, and, being required to submit it to Professor Channing, got only this remark by way of criticism, — "You had better write another poem." "What a useless remark that was!" said Emerson; "he might have pointed out to me some things in my work that were better than others, for all could not have been equally bad." Charles Emerson said, "He did not treat me so unhandsomely; for when I took him a prose exercise once, he said to me, 'Emerson, if Burke had wished to express such a thought as yours, he would have written so-and-so.'" "That was much better," said Waldo Emerson, "for the very name of Burke is inspiring; and what you had written could not have been wholly worthless, if it suggested any comparison with Burke." He was sure he had got little instruction or criticism from his professors that was of value, but he ascribed much to the stimulus and example given by his Aunt Mary. A friend once asked him, "What would have happened in the development of your mind if you had been born and grown up in the small town of Harvard, where your father was first settled as parish minister?" "That circumstance would have made little difference; Nature and books would have been with me." "But what if your Aunt Mary had not taken part in your training?" "Ah, that would have been a loss! she was as great an element in my life as Greece or Rome." He told me once that she was never fairly just to her stepfather, Doctor Ripley, because he could not write well,—being so good a writer herself.

Emerson had preserved the only mention I ever heard of a college duel fought by his uncle, Daniel Bliss Ripley, the doctor's younger son, which caused his expulsion from Harvard, and his withdrawal to Alabama, where, at a town called Saint Stephens, he lived and died, without returning to his native land. "I once saw a letter," said Emerson, "from my father, William Emerson, to George Cabot, the senator, and friend of Washington, asking him to interpose and prevent the duel between his half-brother, Ripley, and young X. But it was impossible to prevent the meeting; they fired one shot each, and the consequence fell heavily on my grandfather."[3] He added that he had once dined at Waltham with Governor Gore, a "great gentleman," and Doctor Ripley's classmate.

I have thus given many samples of Emerson's

[119]

table-talk, and will only add here those which Ellery Channing noted down:—

Foreign Travel.

"It is the American malady,—*lues Americana;* it is the cholera. I have been visiting in the country, as I thought,—and behold, a lady, a professor's wife in a little college, began to talk to me about the Bernese Alps! The Americans are wretched, go where they will. George Bradford was miserable in Europe; he had left Rome and gone to Paris without a reason, save that others were going; and now he wished to go back. I do not know that he should have gone even to Rome; that is something exceptional. Paris does not seem good till you have left it."

George Sand.

"I have already lost her. According to my comprehension, good taste does not consist in magnifying the little, as she does, but in the selection of good things that can be properly magnified."

Burns.

"I was greatly surprised at the applause that greeted my speech at the Burns dinner in Boston the other day. Not having had a very good opinion of this Scottish songster, I renewed my acquaintance with him by a fresh reading, and to a better purpose. But I had only a few moments to prepare myself for speaking."

Tennyson.

"Walking out in the autumnal woods this afternoon with George Bradford, he thought that all *Maud* was filled with descriptions of these golden colors; but when he looked in the book he found only these two lines,

'And out he walked when the wind like a broken worldling wailed,
And the flying gold of the ruined woodlands drove thro' the air.'

Tennyson has not the fulness of Wordsworth. Milton would have hardly lifted his eyelids to see such things as *Maud.* Yet these Idylls of his show that the Ideal may still be built in England."

Reading.

"I like reading as well as ever I did in my youth. That is one thing that has lost no charm

[121]

for me. Give me my book and candle, and I am alone with the universe."

Writing
(Said of a course of Lectures repeated).

"All I have learned of writing is to scratch out a little. I have learned to omit the word 'very.' These published discourses of mine do not read as they did when they were delivered, so many years ago,—fourteen years, is it? Yes, I have that vanity of Doctor Ripley, who used without fail to read his sermons over to the family after the service in the afternoon. And so I repeat my old discourses."

Future Life.

"I think well of Goethe's saying,—that if Nature has given us these faculties, and I have employed mine well, and faithfully to the end, she is bound still further to explain the questions which they put."

Of a Little Lady.

"She is such a perfect little Serenity! 'Her Serene Lowness,' we might call her."

Parker Pillsbury, the Abolitionist Orator.

"He lives in the other Concord, our New Hampshire namesake, and has much of the New Hampshire vigor about him. He talks well in his chair, but does not read as well from his paper."

Richard Cobden.

"I dined with Mr. Cobden at John Forbes's in Milton the other day, but he did not speak much directly. I saw he had the true English feeling, and was talking aside about his six per cents. He spoke interrogatively, and I thought was growing seedy. I asked him why he did not let us make an occasion for him to speak; but he said when he came over it was to keep his ears open and his mouth shut."[4]

Nirvana.

"Different persons among the Buddhists take their special views of the meaning of the doctrine of Nirvana. They have their Kants and Hegels, of course, who make each his own interpretation."

Sickness.

"James Burke, my man, when he is sick is

spleeny. He thinks he shall die, that he cannot earn half his wages, must go to his sister,—and it is all very dreadful. Strange how differently people view their colics and belly-aches! Some laugh at their dumps, and see the joke, as they should. Mrs. A and Mrs. B really believe that they are ill; and I have no doubt it is true for the moment. But let anything occur to tempt Mrs. B out, and she goes at once."

Debt.

"When my debts begin to grow clamorous I think I must take some means of satisfying them. I have now in my pocket three cents and a counterfeit half-dollar."

To his Publisher
(On being paid twice for the same Essay).

"Mr. Fields! I ought not to take this money; but I was a thief from the foundation of the world."

South Carolina.

"Think of a country where there is but one opinion! where there is no minority. Fisher Ames was right in saying that the best majority was where there was but one over,—that is, where opinion was most evenly divided."

This remark about South Carolina, of which it used to be said that "when Calhoun took snuff, the whole State sneezed," was not made in 1844, at the time of Samuel Hoar's expulsion from Charleston, but later, in connection with the outbreak of the Civil War, in which, from first to last, Emerson took the side of Union and Liberty. But in connection with Mr. Hoar's affair, a characteristic citation may be given. Ellery Channing, writing from New York in the winter of 1844–45, had inquired of Emerson if the conduct of the "old Squire" (as he was called in Concord) had been quite brave enough in withdrawing. To this Emerson gave substantially the same reply which he gave to Channing's friend, S. G. Ward, as printed in the little volume, *Letters from Emerson to a Friend*, four years ago. He said (December 17, 1844):—

"Mr. Hoar has just come home from Carolina, and gave me this morning a narrative of his visit.

He has behaved admirably well, I judge. One expression struck me, which he said he regretted a little, afterwards, as it might sound a little vaporing. A gentleman who was very much his friend called him into a private room to say that the danger from the populace had increased so much that he must now insist on Mr. Hoar's leaving the city at once; and he showed him where he might procure a carriage, and where he might safely stop on the way to his plantation, which he would reach the next morning. Mr. Hoar thanked him, but told him again that he could not and would not go,—and that he had rather his broken skull should be carried to Massachusetts by somebody else, than to carry it home safe himself whilst his duty required him to remain. He did not consent to depart, but in every instance refused,—to the sheriff, and acting mayor, to his friends, and to the Committee of the South Carolina Association,—and only went when they came in crowds with carriages to conduct him to the boat, and go he must. Then he got into the coach himself, not thinking it proper to be dragged."

It must be remembered that this venerable gentleman was in Charleston as the envoy of Massachusetts, to protest against the imprisonment of her free colored seamen, while their vessel lay in port,—so fearful were the proud gentry of that State lest the contagion of liberty might be communicated to their slaves. Poetic justice required that the insult to Massachusetts, and to Kansas in 1856, should be requited in less than twenty years by the presence in South Carolina of Colonel Higginson's black regiment, recruited from slaves, and of Colonel Montgomery's soldiers, also recruited from slaves. Emerson viewed this recompense with satisfaction; and when, a few years earlier, I had carried Captain Montgomery, then a Kansas partisan leader, to his house, he received the gallant descendant of the Scotch Montgomeries, bearing himself like a French Chevalier, with much hospitality.

Hospitality, in the usual sense, and also in the broader meaning of liberality of soul toward other men's thought, was a distinguishing trait of Emerson. Though far from wealthy, and at times much narrowed in his income by bad investments, his house was open to more guests than any other in Concord, and he also entertained his visitors from a distance very often in Boston. In his earlier acquaintance with Walt Whitman, he desired to bring him to Concord, in the spring of 1860, when Whitman was in Boston, printing a new edition of his *Leaves of Grass;* and Alcott and Henry Thoreau had the same wish, to invite him to their houses. But it was found that Mrs. Emerson, Mrs. Alcott, and Sophia Thoreau were so prejudiced against Whitman by some things in his book, that they would not join in the invitation. Twenty-one years later, in September, 1881, when Whitman did make his only visit to Concord, as my guest, Mrs. Alcott and Miss Thoreau were dead, but Mrs. Emerson came with her husband to an evening conversation at my house, and cordially invited him to dine with her the next day, as he did; and Louisa Alcott, who had much admiration for Whitman, came with her father, and bore her part in the colloquy. Whitman has described this visit in one of his books; it occurred but a few months before Emerson's death. Emerson had told me, long before, that when he proposed to Doctor Holmes and Mr. Longfellow to invite Whitman to one of the monthly dinners of the Boston Saturday Club, of which all three were members, neither of these poets manifested any wish to meet Whitman, and he was not invited.

I have dwelt, in this book, chiefly on personal traits and events well known to me, in the life of this great man, leaving them to bear their own testimony to his character. Fitly to delineate that, on the broader canvas of a biography, though I should wish to do so, would be beyond my powers, as it has proved to be with most who have attempted it. No adequate memoir (though several excellent sketches have appeared) preserves for those who knew him, or for those who read him thoughtfully, his remarkable traits in their completeness; while many writers have misconceived him greatly. Time is needed, even the distance of a century, to show his colossal portraiture in due perspective. One quality in him impressed all who met him: his freedom from the common defects. Henry James, Senior, with his theologic vocabulary, called him "the unfallen man," and Alcott, with others, used the same figure of speech. My dear friend Ednah Cheney, writing to Ariana Walker in 1852, after hearing him in Boston, said: "Emerson's lectures are finished. He never was higher or nobler; never so clear, humane, and practical. He looks like an angel fresh from Paradise, and speaks as if he had never been at the Tower of Babel, but had retained his first heavenly accents." This youthful estimate has a touch of Concord hyperbole, but goes to the root of the matter. He had something in his mind and heart which could so be described. I must say, as did Sir Robert Harley's chaplain of that grand Englishman: "My language is not a match for his excellent virtues: his spiritual lineaments and beauties are above my pencil. I want art to draw his picture."

NOTES

Note 1 (page 29).

Like Emerson's own character, which had surprising contradictions in it, Mary Emerson could be differently viewed from diverse standpoints. A relative of hers, still living, who spent some time with Doctor Ripley in the Old Manse, was about to leave Concord, and her aged kinsman thus addressed her: "I will give you a short lecture, my dear. In your future course of life, remember to follow Duty rather than Inclination; a good rule, of which your Aunt Mary has always held the opposite." She certainly believed that she did her whole duty, however disagreeable it was to others. At her death in May, 1863, in her ninetieth year, I wrote of her in the Boston *Commonwealth* (to which Alcott, Channing, Thoreau, posthumously, and Emerson contributed—the last sparingly): "Her conversation was a singular *mélange* of sincere devotion, worldly wisdom, wit, and anecdote; and she was thought to have the power of saying more disagreeable things in a half-hour than any person living. Reproof was her mission, she thought, and she fulfilled it unsparingly. But she knew how to be tolerant, was a great humorist, and loved to meet forcible persons who would not agree with her." A kinswoman thought a young editor ought not to have told so much truth of the deceased, and complained to Emerson, who read the paragraph, and merely said (as was reported to me by another niece), "I see that he was well acquainted with Aunt Mary."

Note 2 (page 97).

This was said in 1878; but in 1880 he did not remember having read it at all.

NOTES

Note 3 (page 119).

The portrait of this handsome young duellist has long hung in the hall at the Old Manse.

Note 4 (page 123).

Emerson had heard Mr. Cobden in England in 1847, and described the speech in a letter to Thoreau.